NEW DIRECTIONS FOR HIGH

Martin Kramer
EDITOR-IN-CHIEF

Academic Freedom: An Everyday Concern

Ernst Benjamin
American Association of University Professors

Donald R. Wagner
West Georgia College

EDITORS

Number 88, Winter 1994

JOSSEY-BASS PUBLISHERS
San Francisco

ACADEMIC FREEDOM: AN EVERYDAY CONCERN
Ernst Benjamin, Donald R. Wagner (eds.)
New Directions for Higher Education, no. 88
Volume XXII, Number 4
Martin Kramer, Editor-in-Chief

© 1994 by Jossey-Bass Inc., Publishers. All rights reserved.

No part of this issue may be reproduced in any form—except for a brief quotation (not to exceed 500 words) in a review or professional work—without permission in writing from the publishers.

Microfilm copies of issues and articles are available in 16mm and 35mm, as well as microfiche in 105mm, through University Microfilms Inc., 300 North Zeeb Road, Ann Arbor, Michigan 48106-1346.

LC 85-644752   ISSN 0271-0560   ISBN 0-7879-9987-3

NEW DIRECTIONS FOR HIGHER EDUCATION is part of The Jossey-Bass Higher and Adult Education Series and is published quarterly by Jossey-Bass Inc., Publishers, 350 Sansome Street, San Francisco, California 94104-1342 (publication number USPS 990-880). Second-class postage paid at San Francisco, California, and at additional mailing offices. POSTMASTER: Send address changes to New Directions for Higher Education, Jossey-Bass Inc., Publishers, 350 Sansome Street, San Francisco, California 94104-1342.

SUBSCRIPTIONS for 1994 cost $47.00 for individuals and $62.00 for institutions, agencies, and libraries.

EDITORIAL CORRESPONDENCE should be sent to the Editor-in-Chief, Martin Kramer, 2807 Shasta Road, Berkeley, California 94708-2011.

Cover photograph and random dot by Richard Blair/Color & Light © 1990.

Manufactured in the United States of America. Nearly all Jossey-Bass books, jackets, and periodicals are printed on recycled paper that contains at least 50 percent recycled waste, including 10 percent postconsumer waste. Many of our materials are also printed with vegetable-based inks; during the printing process these inks emit fewer volatile organic compounds (VOCs) than petroleum-based inks. VOCs contribute to the formation of smog.

Contents

EDITORS' NOTES 1
Ernst Benjamin, Donald R. Wagner

1. The Freedom to Teach 11
William W. Pendleton
Academic freedom in the classroom is essential to the quality of instruction and learning. Speech codes and assessment mandates, as currently proposed, diminish academic freedom and quality.

2. It's Power, Stupid! 21
Mary W. Gray
Sexual harassment is an abuse of power. It should be prohibited, not through constraints on academic freedom such as speech codes, but through enforcement of ethical professional conduct.

3. *Fischer v. The Medical College of Georgia and the R.J. Reynolds Tobacco Company*: A Case Study of Constraints on Research 33
Paul M. Fischer
Without vigorous protection of academic freedom, corporate power and state action may discourage economically or politically controversial research.

4. Academic Freedom and Artistic Expression 45
Carol Simpson Stern
Artistic expression is often controversial and subject to attack. The protection of academic freedom is essential if the arts are to continue to flourish within the academy.

5. "Dirty Little Cases": Academic Freedom, Governance, and Professionalism 59
Sheila Slaughter
Faculty participation in academic governance is a relatively frequent source of academic freedom disputes. Dismissal of faculty over such issues usually occurs in less prestigious colleges that have less regard for national professional standards.

6. Academic Freedom, Professionalism, and Intramural Speech   77
David M. Rabban
The more directly that faculty speech within the university relates to the faculty's professional responsibilities in advancing knowledge and inquiry, the more it requires academic freedom.

7. Academic Freedom and Regional Accreditation: Guarantors of   89
Quality in the Academy
Sandra E. Elman
Accreditation fosters academic freedom as a condition of academic quality. Accreditation depends on academic freedom to secure reliable institutional self-evaluation and planning.

INDEX   101

Editors' Notes

Academic freedom is widely revered in American higher education. For many, however, it is a Sunday religion. In their view, academic freedom is required only to protect the extraordinary explorer after truth or the rare classroom controversialist. Since academic freedom is essential only to these exceptional searchers after truth, the protection of academic freedom is also exceptional: it may be left to academic good conscience or the courts, and it is not the sort of everyday concern that requires the systematic institutional protection of tenure. Since most faculty members are not exceptional, they have no need of academic freedom and, accordingly, no need other than economic self-interest to justify tenure.

The essays in this journal offer a more comprehensive understanding of academic freedom. They show that academic freedom is integral to the everyday professional lives of faculty, their students, and their colleges and universities. They recognize that ordinary, as well as extraordinary, teaching, research, and collegial conduct may create controversy, and that the commonplace ideas of the campus do not always correspond with the common-sense view of the community. Indeed, today's campus is itself a complex community, where interest groups as well as ideas contend, and decisions reflect bureaucratic and financial priorities as well as educational concerns. In these circumstances, academic freedom provides the faculty employed by these complex institutions with the professional autonomy that is essential to fulfill their daily academic responsibilities with professional integrity.

Kingman Brewster, former president of Yale University, provides a classic expression of the everyday perspective on academic freedom in this contrast of external and internal threats: "The dramatic image of the university under siege from taxpayers, politicians, or even occasional alumni is a vivid, but not the most difficult, aspect of the pressures which tend to erode academic freedom. The more subtle condition of academic freedom is that faculty members, once they have proven their potential during a period of junior probation, should not feel beholden to *anyone,* especially Department Chairmen, Deans, Provosts, or Presidents, for favor, let alone for survival. . . . In strong universities, assuring freedom from intellectual conformity coerced within the institution is even more of a concern than is the protection of freedom from external interference" (Brewster, 1972, p. 382). The essays in this collection discuss precisely the sort of less publicly visible, daily academic matters that might be, and too often are, subject to internal pressures for intellectual conformity in the absence of respect for academic freedom.

Internal pressures for conformity may come from students and colleagues as well as from administrators. This stems in part from the fact that many faculty members do not themselves perceive the everyday significance of academic freedom. Edward Shils has recently observed in connection with extramural threats to academic freedom that "[m]ost academics have not and do not give much thought to academic freedom. For many of them it has not been an issue at all. They did not dream of doing any of the things which might have been the object of sanctions and for which the protection of academic freedom would have been adduced. They have usually been indifferent when sanctions were visited on a colleague in some remote department for having expressed himself outside the university on some political or social issue" (Shils, 1993, p. 204).

Professor Shils further observes that this lack of collegial support may derive from an absence of sympathy or from disagreement as well as from thoughtlessness. He notes that external demands increasingly have their internal collegial enforcers: "Infringements on academic freedom are nowadays, to a greater extent, infringements imposed from within the university and even from within the teaching staff" (p. 206).

Professor Shils is concerned that federal policies, especially affirmative action policies, may be applied in a manner that is inimicable to academic freedom. Though there is much disagreement concerning the precise boundaries between appropriate and inappropriate federal intervention to ensure equal opportunity, it is essential to recognize that daily threats to academic freedom proceed from such benign intentions. While xenophobia, bigotry, and political extremism—or even political convention—do continue to challenge free expression from time to time, everyday threats to academic freedom more often proceed from good intentions. For example, there is nothing inherently wrong, and much that is good, about the contending views in the current curricular debate: students should know more about the landmarks of their own culture and society as well as acquire a deeper understanding of cultures other than their own. The threat to academic freedom here lies not in the alternative educational ideals, but in the decision-making process. To the extent that this process relies on political constraints—from within the academy or from society—rather than collegial professional deliberation grounded in a proper respect for the university's societal and intellectual responsibilities, academic freedom is lost and academic integrity eroded.

Constraints may be subtle, and it is often difficult to distinguish legitimate from illegitimate demands. It is extraordinarily difficult at times to determine whether a decision about tenure or promotion reflects proper concerns about merit, disputable concerns about programmatic relevance, or outright bias based on race, gender, or ideology. For example, one may have to ascertain on a case-by-case basis whether the high esteem accorded publication in certain mainstream journals and the relative lack of esteem for publication in some women's or ethnic studies journals rest on these journals' academic merits, on majority convention, or on simple bias. Collegial judgment is essential to such determinations—and collegial judgement itself may err. Nevertheless, such everyday judgments ultimately determine the climate for academic freedom.

Many questions concerning academic freedom arise during periods of fiscal constraint. Administrators and faculty members need to make difficult and inherently controversial decisions to ensure their institution's fiscal health. It is often difficult, for example, to ensure that the selection of programs for termination genuinely rests on appropriate qualitative and financial criteria rather than on improper bias against individual faculty members or programs. Similarly, it is sometimes difficult to determine whether faculty critiques of university expenditures proceed from vital educational concerns—in which case the protection of the faculty's professional expression is essential—or simply from financial self-interest or disgruntlement. Whatever the precise boundaries of academic freedom in such matters, it is important to recognize that sound academic judgement on these difficult issues requires intellectual independence and an opportunity for collegial deliberation. Academic freedom is not a Sunday ideal that institutions may set aside in difficult times or subordinate to more practical matters. Academic freedom is itself the practical prerequisite for sound academic performance and policy making.

The essays that follow provide both detailed consideration of the daily, practical contribution of academic freedom to university life and careful consideration of the appropriate relationship between academic freedom and other essential academic concerns. The essays do not catalogue the entire range of specific academic freedom concerns. [For additional perspectives with a greater emphasis on legal issues, see the essays in the recent *Texas Law Review* ("Symposium on Academic Freedom," 1988), and the special issue of *Law and Contemporary Problems* ("Freedom and Tenure in the Academy," 1993).] They do explore examples of the major types of issues that arise with respect to the three principal professional activities of the faculty: teaching, research, and service. The first two essays deal primarily with faculty-student relationships, the next two with research and creative activity, and the final three with the faculty's role in academic governance. But the topics of the essays, like faculty activities themselves, often cut across these boundaries. And even though our essayists share a commitment to academic freedom, they do not always agree about its application to specific problems.

Academic freedom is often identified only with the obvious issues of subject matter and ideological perspective—such as the teaching of Marxism or creationism—which are actually relatively infrequent sources of friction. Because these important issues are widely recognized, the essays included here focus on the more subtle, and more pervasive, issues that arise in the teaching process regardless of subject matter or perspective. Similarly, precisely because it is widely recognized, we do not address in this collection the most highly debated process issue of all, the debate over classroom advocacy. The editors agree with Matthew Finken that "subject to a professional obligation to state opposing views fairly (analogous to the requirement in research that the evidence not be distorted) and to treat with respect students who disagree, the teacher is free passionately to espouse controversial views that are germane to the subject" (Finken, 1988, p. 88).

The essays included here share a similar, if less obvious, concern for the mutual rights and obligations of faculty and students. The faculty's academic freedom in the classroom, after all, not only originates in and must contribute to the scholarly development of the faculty, but is founded upon and must contribute to the academic development and freedom of the student (Benjamin, 1992).

In Chapter One of this collection, William Pendleton explores two current practices wherein the desire to protect students may lead to actions that erode academic freedom and, in turn, student learning. First he discusses the way in which "speech codes" and other practices intended to protect students from racial, gender, or ethnic slurs or harassment may instead improperly limit the manner and substance of classroom presentations. He then considers how the growing requirement for outcomes assessments diminishes faculty authority over course content and presentation. It is especially important that he founds his discussion on a recognition of the multiple aspects of instruction, which include not only course content but also the methodology of inquiry and the instructor's pedagogical perspective. Differences in faculty members' teaching styles and objectives merit protection, at a minimum, because students also vary greatly in their learning styles and objectives. Pedagogical orthodoxy threatens student learning as much as it does freedom of instruction.

In Chapter Two, Mary Gray reminds us, however, that academic freedom does not protect faculty exploitation or harassment of students. Such unprofessional conduct is an abuse of power rather than a legitimate exercise of authority, and it does not merit the protection accorded to proper professional conduct. This does not mean it is appropriate to regulate the content of classroom presentations. It does mean, however, that the right of faculty members to challenge their students, or even confront them vigorously with uncomfortable ideas, does not give them a license for abuse. Similarly, although many faculty members and students value a warm, personal teaching style and may even form lasting friendships, this does not translate into a right to exploit professional authority and prestige for personal or sexual advantage.

The precise boundaries of appropriate conduct are not easily drawn. Difficult cases may require collegial, peer evaluation. Comparison of the essays by Professors Gray and Pendleton should, however, illustrate the way in which the teaching process is deeply dependent on the protected but professionally responsible exercise of academic freedom.

Academic freedom is frequently identified most directly with the untrammeled pursuit of truth in faculty research. Basic research is rarely restricted by doctrinal or ideological concerns, although such concerns have affected even scientific issues, such as medical research on fetal tissue or survey research on sexual attitudes and conduct. Basic research is commonly shaped by governmental, corporate, and foundation funding preferences. Such economic pressures affect applied research even more directly and pervasively. Faculty members often agree to focus on a specific topic or pursue a desired solution understanding and accepting such limitations, but they also assume that research will be performed in a manner consistent with professional standards of integrity.

Where research—whether pure or applied—has a direct and controversial effect, it may prompt serious adverse consequences. Ibsen's "Enemy of the People," who suffers dismissal and ostracism for the elementary discovery that the water in a resort's baths is polluted, provides an excellent, if nonacademic, example. Dr. Paul Fischer's legal battle, described in Chapter Three, resulting from his research on the effects of cigarette advertising on children, is a useful contemporary illustration of the problem. Neither the tobacco company's request for the evidence for his findings nor his university's compliance with the state Open Records Act were inherently wrong. But the ability of a large corporation through litigation to discourage research that is damaging to its business—no matter how beneficial that research may be to consumers—coupled with the timidity of the university faced with this problem provides a compelling example of the threats to academic freedom, even for research that is neither scientifically innovative nor ideologically controversial.

Controversy surrounding artistic exploration and expression is more commonly anticipated. Even so, those who regard academic freedom as narrowly concerned with the pursuit of knowledge sometimes tend to neglect the issue of freedom of artistic expression; some would even say that artistic freedom is not truly a matter of academic concern. But the arts flourish in the university, and to an extent they flourish because of it. Carol Simpson Stern's essay, in Chapter Four, explains how deeply artistic exploration and expression depend on academic freedom. In doing so, Stern helps us understand the close interrelation between inquiry and expression. She reminds us that those who would limit the protections of academic freedom solely to the quest for truth fail to recognize that the academic enterprise should and does encompass diverse forms of inquiry and expression.

The remaining essays provide a much-needed exploration of the contributions of academic freedom to faculty participation in academic governance. The American Association of University Professors (AAUP) has, since its inception in 1915, extended the concept of academic freedom to embrace extramural faculty discourse. Faculty should certainly enjoy the rights of free speech accorded all other citizens, and lawful extramural speech has been explicitly included within the compass of academic freedom ("1940 Statement of Principles," 1990). The AAUP has also sought, on a case-by-case basis and without issuing a general statement on the issue, to protect *intra*mural faculty speech on matters extending beyond immediate research and teaching concerns. Good universities have, themselves, generally offered a wide latitude for debate rather than risk constraints on the professional contributions of faculty members. It is prudent to provide this protection, since critiques of unprotected faculty speech may serve as a pretext for silencing their protected speech.

Nonetheless, the protection of academic freedom in respect to faculty participation in academic governance needs, and is only just beginning to receive, specific and careful support. Professor Shils offers a useful summation:

> Academic freedom is also the right of the academic to participate in those activities within the university which affect directly the performance of academic things. The right to participate in these activities also carries with it the obligation to do so. The privilege of academic freedom confers the rights and imposes the obligations of academic citizenship. In the first instance, this includes the rights and obligations of the academic to participate in the decisions regarding the appointment of teachers and research workers who will work in his or her own department. It also includes the right and obligation to participate in decisions regarding the substance and form of courses of study, examinations, the marking of examinations, and the awarding of degrees. At this point, academic freedom becomes the right and obligation to participate in academic self-government [Shils, 1993, p. 190].

It is noteworthy that Professor Shils regards faculty participation in self-governance as an obligation as well as a right. The AAUP has long included participation in governance among faculty obligations in its "Statement on Professional Ethics" (1990), even as it includes the right of such participation in its "Statement on Government of Colleges and Universities."

What has heretofore been too-much neglected, and has now been asserted by Professor Shils and formally elaborated for the first time by the AAUP (in June 1994), is that the faculty right and obligation to participate in governance carries with it the protections of academic freedom ("On the Relationship of Faculty Governance to Academic Freedom," 1994). The essay by Sheila Slaughter (Chapter Five) documents the need for such protection in detail by describing a series of AAUP investigations that turned primarily on governance issues. She adopts the term "dirty little cases" to describe the subject of these investigations because they were characterized by the absence of professional recognition and respect. These are the everyday conflicts in the academy, far more common than those cases that arise from doctrinal or ideological disputes. As Slaughter also shows, there is a strong association between the denial of professional respect and a lack of academic standing of the institution involved.

The importance of delineating the interrelation between academic freedom and faculty governance derives not only from the frequency with which these problems occur in the academy and their consequences for institutional quality, but also from the absence of careful analysis of the issue. David Rabban provides this careful analysis in Chapter Six. Those who confuse academic freedom with freedom of expression sometimes neglect a vital distinction: freedom of expression is a civic right of the individual, providing protection against state action; academic freedom, by contrast, is the right of faculty, as officers or employees of their institutions and irrespective of constitutional guarantees, to protection against institutional or employer sanctions—regardless of whether the institution is a state or private employer. Academic freedom includes, and in governance matters often turns upon, the right of faculty members to disagree publicly with their institutional employers, including not only the chairs, deans, provosts, and presidents mentioned by President Brewster, but even the governing boards.

Rabban perceptively explores this unique right. He reviews a wide range of topics that have occasioned controversy, showing how many of them involve professional issues important to the quality of education. He shows that many institutional issues that extend beyond the direct activities of teaching and research nonetheless require faculty members' professional judgment. He argues that the protection of intramural faculty speech is, therefore, essential to the professional performance of the faculty and consequently the quality of the institution.

He also emphasizes, however, that the unqualified defense of any and all faculty speech in the name of academic freedom would weaken both the claim of academic freedom and respect for professional judgement. Faculty complaints about their employment situation that are motivated by self-interest or disgruntlement—though deserving of the same protections accorded similar expressions by other, nonacademic, employees—do not deserve the special protections afforded by academic freedom. The fact that academic freedom is an everyday matter does not mean that everything faculty members wish to assert merits its specific protections. Since academic freedom is grounded in the professional obligations of the faculty, its primary protections apply to professional matters.

Sandra Elman's essay (Chapter Seven) on the relationship between academic freedom and accreditation concludes the volume with a broad consideration of how and why accreditation protects academic freedom across the full range of faculty members' professional activities. She discusses the vital role of faculty independence in shaping and attaining the institutional mission. At its core, however, her essay concerns the role of academic freedom in shared governance, and it explores the essential role of faculty independence and expression in ensuring the quality of accreditation reviews. Her discussions of assessment and governance also emphasize the need to balance and integrate faculty judgment with that of administrators and others responsible for university affairs.

All these essays share the view that academic freedom is an everyday necessity for professional excellence in teaching, scholarship, and service to the university and the community. Each author also recognizes—as Gray, Rabban, and Elman emphasize— that since the right of academic freedom rests on professional need, academic freedom entails professional responsibility and applies primarily to professional conduct. The obligations of professional responsibility are clearly articulated in the classic "1940 Statement of Principles on Academic Freedom and Tenure." As teachers, faculty are admonished "not to introduce into their teaching controversial matter which has no relation to their subject." Also, faculty are cautioned that, "as scholars and educational officers," they "should at all times be accurate, should exercise appropriate restraint, should show respect for the opinion of others, and should make every effort to indicate they are not speaking for the institution" ("1940 Statement of Principles . . . ," 1990, pp. 3–4).

The interdependence of academic freedom and academic responsibility does not mean that a professional lapse or wrong can be made right by the further wrong of a denial of academic freedom. It does mean that egregious or substantial and persistent professional misconduct, including expressive misconduct, should be subject to institutional sanctions, up to and including dismissal, following administration demonstration of adequate cause before a body of faculty peers for major sanctions and affordance of a grievance procedure for minor sanctions ("Recommended Institutional Regulations . . . ," 1990). Unprofessional behavior, such as slander, plagiarism, or harassment, cannot claim the protection of academic freedom merely because it happens to involve speech or writing. Professional behavior rightly claims the protections of academic freedom not only in the interest of the search for truth and in creative expression, but also to protect the discourse essential to achieving the highest possible academic standards.

The protection of academic freedom requires more than reverence for the ideal. We believe the essays in this volume provide detailed support for the proposition that the ideal of academic freedom would not long survive the hurly-burly of university life without the institutional support provided by the system of peer review and tenure. It is essential to recognize, as is particularly evident in the essays by Rabban and Slaughter, that even though most challenges to academic freedom do not involve great clashes of principle (and all too often seem like "dirty little cases"), these challenges are threats to more than faculty members' economic well-being or job security. They are threats to the professional integrity that is essential to academic judgment and to the intellectual independence essential to academic discourse and discoveries.

We may properly ensure the quality of faculty work by distinguishing professional from unprofessional behavior, respecting the former and discouraging the latter. It is not possible to selectively ensure academic freedom for the most compelling cases if academic freedom, and the professional practice and habits of mind on which it rests, are eroded daily and celebrated only on Sunday. Academic freedom is the only atmosphere in which academic work can flourish. If we do not conserve and protect it, our daily work will be stunted and we will falter when great tasks confront us.

This volume's editors and most of its contributors have served as members and leaders of the AAUP. Our understanding of academic freedom benefits from our knowledge of AAUP policy and our experience of AAUP work. Our presentations are, however, our own, and apart from direct quotations from AAUP policy statements, these essays do not necessarily reflect the official views of the AAUP.

Ernst Benjamin
Donald R. Wagner
Editors

References

Benjamin, E. "Freedom in the Classroom." In W. A. Bryan and R. H. Mullendore (eds.), *Rights, Freedoms, and Responsibilities of Students*. New Directions for Student Services, no. 59. San Francisco: Jossey-Bass, 1992.

Brewster, K., Jr. "On Tenure." *AAUP Bulletin*, Winter 1972, pp. 381–383.

Finken, M. "The Tenure System." In A. L. Deneef, C. D. Goodwin, and E. S. McCrate (eds.), *The Academic's Handbook*. Durham, N.C.: Duke University Press, 1988.

"Freedom and Tenure in the Academy" [symposium]. *Law and Contemporary Problems*, 1993 (entire issue).

"1940 Statement of Principles on Academic Freedom and Tenure." In *AAUP Policy Documents and Reports*. Washington, D.C.: American Association of University Professors, 1990, pp. 3–10.

"On the Relationship of Faculty Governance to Academic Freedom." *Academe*, Jul.–Aug. 1994, pp. 47–49.

"Recommended Institutional Regulations on Academic Freedom and Tenure." In *AAUP Policy Documents and Reports*. Washington, D.C.: American Association of University Professors, 1990, pp. 21–30.

Shils, E. "Do We Still Need Academic Freedom?" *The American Scholar*, Spring 1993, pp. 187–209.

"Statement on Government of Colleges and Universities." In *AAUP Policy Documents and Reports*. Washington, D.C.: American Association of University Professors, 1990, pp. 119–124.

"Statement on Professional Ethics." In *AAUP Policy Documents and Reports*. Washington, D.C.: American Association of University Professors, 1990, pp. 75–76.

"Symposium on Academic Freedom." *Texas Law Review*, 1988, 66 (7), 1247–1659.

ERNST BENJAMIN *serves on the professional staff of the American Association of University Professors, where he was general secretary from 1984 to 1994. He taught and held various administrative positions at Wayne State University from 1965 to 1984.*

DONALD R. WAGNER *is professor of political science and director of the honors program at West Georgia College. He has been executive secretary of the Georgia Conference of the American Association of University Professors since 1982.*

Speech codes and assessment mandates diminish academic freedom and, thereby, the quality of teaching and learning.

The Freedom to Teach

William W. Pendleton

Academic freedom in the classroom is not merely a matter of constitutional free speech, nor should it be regarded as a privilege of the faculty. It is a fundamental requisite of effective education. It rests not on a simplistic assumption that anything may be said or taught in any class; rather, it rests on the assumption regarding the professional competence and integrity of the faculty. Ultimately it disallows the intrusion of others, regardless of their intentions or competence, in the conduct of courses. Academic freedom does not ensure perfect or even the best possible education in every class. But it is the best means of ensuring that, over the course of a student's career, he or she receives an education that is broad, flexible, nondoctrinaire, and subject to the self-correction inherent in exposing students to many teachers, all free to pursue the pedagogy and content of their classes as they judge best.

Accepting academic freedom requires accepting that some will not teach so well as others think they should, nor will classes on the same subjects cover or give equal emphasis to the same topics. A common purpose is attained through the individual faculty members' experience, their previous education, and their interactions with other members of their discipline and with the many committees on teaching and academic standards within their department, university, and professional organizations.

This system has served higher education well. Efforts to depart from it for religious, political, or social regulatory purposes have been, for the most part, detrimental to excellence; with the passage of time, such efforts have come to be seen as ludicrous by subsequent generations of scholars. Religious dogmatism in history or sociology, creationism, Lysenkoism—the list could be continued—when made a matter of external control rather than of internal debate, have had a damaging impact on the advancement of knowledge. When left to free examination, these systems of thought have assumed a proper place in human understanding.

Yet the temptation remains to make things "better" by imposing controls on the classroom. Should not students be free from error in instruction? Should not students be free from fear, confusion, intimidation, and belittlement? Should not universities protect students from improper views, outdated theories, and distorted data? If faculty remain free to teach as they wish, will they not release evils of the worst sort on the impressionable young? These questions are raised repeatedly, as they should be. But the too-frequent answers—add new administrative powers, allow intrusion into the classroom, provide for regulation of faculty by persons little qualified for the task—are supplied because they are easy and they appeal to those who little understand education.

Academic Freedom and Instruction

There are two kinds of academic freedom; they impact teaching in different and, to a degree, contradictory ways. The first is the freedom of faculty members to follow their personal and professional ethics in presenting courses without restraint or direction imposed by outside agencies. The second is the freedom of institutions of higher education to organize and offer a curriculum without interference from other parts of society, especially the government. Each of these freedoms is vital to effective education. Each imposes obligations on the faculty and the university. Each is constrained and influenced in its exercise by many other forces in the broader society.

This essay examines two current movements in academe with a view to the threat they pose to academic freedom and therefore to effective education in colleges and universities. These movements are the result of efforts to deal with real problems, but they suffer from a lack of academic purpose, scholarly direction, and educational integrity. They are the efforts to impose speech codes to prevent possible offense to certain protected classes of people, and similarly motivated efforts to devise new means of assessing faculty members. In both cases the results have been antithetical to effective education, even though the efforts are rooted in good intentions to implement worthy goals. The results have been unfortunate because these efforts are largely the work of nonacademicians: they are based on false assumptions about the educational process, and they ignore existing and alternative methods of obtaining the desired results which do not share the shortcomings of the controlled speech and assessment movements.

In order fully to appreciate the impact of these forces on higher education, it is useful to consider three aspects of instruction: the formal content of courses, the implied basis of understanding that characterizes all learning, and the ancillary instruction that is a part of any course. Briefly, the formal content of a course is its specific subject matter—history, calculus, and so on— including content and methodologies appropriate to the field. The implied basis of understanding refers to the use of evidence, authority, logic, and inference, as well as to the paradigms students can deduce from the manner in which course materials are presented. Ancillary instruction refers to the instructor's attitude toward knowledge—its joys or miseries—and his or her personal relationship with the content of the course in life.

Some courses may emphasize certain of these aspects more than others. In some courses the logic of inference may be part of the formal content, for example. But the critical point is that a complete education of the student must include all three aspects, often within the classroom. Personal anecdotes from the instructor may underscore and make more memorable the course's formal content. Irrational authority in the presentation may belie the rigorous logic of the formal content of the course. The able teacher exposes students to all three aspects of learning while developing their understanding and scholarly character. It is only through all three that education, as opposed to training, takes place.

Whatever interferes with these processes constrains education. Speech codes and assessment currently in force at many colleges and universities directly impinge on all three of these areas, and especially on the second and third areas, where the core of an educated mind is developed. For that reason they are dangerous to education. Too often such forces act to contradict the fundamental tenets of scholarship, so that *miseducation* is encouraged. Authority, rather than reason and evidence, becomes the basis for selecting subjects; a popular, homogenized understanding, rather than a variety of interpretations, determines the content of the course.

Speech Codes

Efforts to impose speech codes at many universities are well known to most academicians. The genesis of these codes is important because it shows the mentality behind them. There has been no crisis of harassment, oral or otherwise, on American campuses. Indeed, proponents of speech codes have had to resort to absurdly inclusive definitions of harassment in order to *manufacture* a crisis. Even saying "women do not do as well as men in this course" has been described as potential harassment (by creating a hostile environment). "Being too friendly," "Unwanted displays of pornographic pictures, posters, cartoons," "Jokes or remarks that are stereotypical" are lumped together with "criminal touching" as potential sexual harassment (for examples of these and other definitions, see Fitzgerald, 1987, p. 33; Leonard and others, 1993, p. 74). Aside from trivializing actual harassment, such definitions suggest an inquisition in search of a crime rather than a considered effort to eliminate injustice.

At Emory University, the first procedures promulgated to deal with harassment allowed that the aggrieved party and the director of the affirmative action office would each appoint two members to a committee, those four would appoint a fifth member, and this committee would then determine guilt and recommend punishment for a faculty member charged with harassment. The absurdity of such a procedure led to its elimination, but for a time it was policy. Even now, the procedure for investigating harassment requires that the investigating committee, after being empaneled, must be specially trained in the nature of harassment. Presumably the faculty members appointed to the committee are not sufficiently aware of what harassment is to recognize it, but other faculty are expected to be sufficiently aware of it not to do it in the first place, lest they be subjected to serious penalties.

Given the penchant of the professional enforcers of speech codes for finding harassment in innocuous remarks, the result can only be a chilling self-censorship by the faculty, or a source of cheap revenge for those who, for whatever reasons, dislike a faculty member. These are not fanciful concerns. The list of serious disruptions of the lives and activities of faculty members by such enforcers, under the pretext of preventing harassment, is too long to be dismissed as a few aberrations (see Coleman, 1990–91; Jacobs, 1993; Thernstrom, 1990–91; and Gross, 1989 for some examples and reactions). Moreover, such disruptions are often based on the most egregious and strained definitions of harassment.

A recent case shows that the problem is not abating. Professor J. Donald Silva was suspended by the University of New Hampshire for sexual harassment, and his pay was cut off after a "student-led tribunal" found him guilty. His crime? In a technical writing class, he likened *focus* to *sex* and quoted Little Egypt on belly dancing to illustrate a simile. A federal judge has ordered his reinstatement. The university is considering whether to appeal (Honan, 1994, p. 19). The problem here is as much with the procedures as with the codes. Are these really serious offenses? Is it really a great offense to use "Oriental" rather than "Asian," "Indian" rather than "Native American" (a designation that is linguistically contorted), "girl" rather than "woman" in reference to females barely past puberty? Are we moving toward classrooms where mentioning steaks might cause a Hindu to feel uncomfortable, saying "PMS" might cause some women to be uncomfortable, having too many references to people of the wrong religion, sex, race, military service history, physical capacity, sexual preference, or what have you can render someone uncomfortable and thus spark a charge of creating a hostile environment, followed by a star-chamber proceeding? We are certainly far enough along that path to be concerned.

When we abandon the informal sanctions that support good taste and well-mannered behavior and confuse abuse with offense, we have moved along a path the can lead to arbitrary decisions about faculty members. When we allow that process to be directed by nonacademicians with little understanding or regard for the subtleties of education, we risk vitally important things in order to prevent trivial offenses. At the same time, we are teaching at other levels lessons that should not be taught. We are suggesting that the "protected classes" are too delicate to defend themselves against insult, that they are incompetent to avail themselves of the protection offered everyone else. That is not a message I would want to convey.

In response to these codes we may increasingly avoid matters of controversy, which is where our best intellectual efforts should be directed. Shall we not discuss racial and sexual differences and the basis for evaluating them unless we first make sure no one will be offended? Education may often be offensive when it is most effective. Should that be lost, what will remain? Shall we be satisfied with the comfortable pablum that offends no one?

The issue here is not solely that of "political correctness" or some new Victorianism. The case of Pauline Bart, who was forced out of her position at the University of Illinois, Chicago, on a harassment claim filed by a male student with the help of the affirmative action office, and that of David Ayers and John Jeffrey, who were fired by Dallas Baptist University, indicate that all parts of the political and ideological spectrum can be adversely affected by these policies. Bart is an outspoken feminist, Ayers an adamant critic of feminism. Jeffrey was a courageous dean who refused to persecute Ayers (Salemi, 1992). Here we are faced with administrative structures and procedures that threaten the heart of academic freedom and from which no one is safe.

The revised policy of Emory University asserts that "the scholarly, educational, or artistic content of any written, oral or other presentation or inquiry shall not be limited by this policy.... This provision shall be liberally construed but shall not be used as a pretextual basis for violation of this policy" ("Formal Procedures...," 1991). One hand giveth, the other taketh away. The procedures will allow those involved to determine, on the basis of their courage and character and instructions from the affirmative action office, if some behavior has a pretextual basis. Surely that is a decision that should be wholly in the hands of the faculty and subject to a clear agreement on what constitutes pretext.

Assessment

Concerns over the effectiveness of higher education have lead to an increasing emphasis on the formal assessment of teaching, learning, and the institutions themselves. In many instances assessment is a legislative mandate. In other cases it is mandated by the trustees or administration of a university. Recently the Department of Education, acting under congressional instruction to control waste in support funds for students, has given major stimulus to the assessment of education on the nation's campuses. The implications for academic freedom are huge, at both the institutional and classroom levels. The mechanism for executing these assessments is found in the accrediting agencies. Difficulties with the law were well discussed in several articles in *Academe* (Longanecker, 1994; Warren, 1994; Tobin, 1994; Benjamin, 1994).

Many instructors have long used some procedure to assess their students' reactions to courses. Often they use supplementary instruments or forms, as well as those provided by their institution. Most faculty members know the shortcomings of these procedures, as well as their usefulness. Traditionally these evaluations have played little if any role in the allocation of resources within the university. Their use has been primarily to provide the faculty member with information about the reaction of students to a course. The assessment movement that has developed during the past ten years has emphasized the use of such procedures for administrative as well as pedagogic purposes. Most academicians are unaware of the extent and potential impact of the assessment movement in higher education. To some the label "movement" might seem extreme. It is not.

The keynote address by Theodore J. Marchese at the American Association of Higher Education's Eighth Conference on Assessment in Higher Education reflects a movement in the first stage of consolidation, where the naive enthusiasm of the initial stage of the movement is treated with tolerant amusement, and the important work that was begun is seen with greater understanding. It would be unfair to some of the participants to characterize the conference in a few paragraphs, especially when they could only attend some of the sessions and only a dozen were available on tape. There is no denying a seriousness of purpose and a great sense of commitment on the part of the conference's attendees.

The tone of a session organized by Tom Angelo represents the strengths and weaknesses of the movement. Angelo summarized the influence of assessment in terms of no great cost and little or no gain (Angelo, 1993). Especially with respect to learning, the movement thus far seems to have had little impact. That may be less surprising in light of the fact that what students have learned was not an important part of the conference. A formulation of "higher-order thinking" set in opposition to "facts and principles" was often drawn without the need to relate higher-order thinking to facts and principles—the essence of most courses. Indeed, syllabi, examinations, and student performance on examinations and other exercises—which form the basis on which most faculty assess their efforts and those of students—seem of little importance to the assessment movement. Involving faculty in the efforts of this movement is given lip service, as well as some real effort (if the reports are accepted at face value).

Yet, why faculty should *want* to be involved in this movement is not examined. What is lacking is an appreciation of the intrusion of the assessors into the activities of the faculty, who are already assessing—and assessing well. If education is to be improved, only faculty in the disciplines concerned are able to make such assessments. One cannot escape the impression that much of the assessment movement behaves like children who have found some important ideas and play delightedly with them without regard to the complex set of ideas that underlie them in the adult world. Too often we encounter educationese that obscures clear thought, confounds the rules of grammar, and reflects an ignorance of the scholarship that must underlie effective education. Though the conference contained much that was of value, the separation of assessment from content and the suggestion that faculty are ineffective and in need of help and direction seem unlikely to gain cooperation from any but the most insecure faculty members or to lead to more effective education. Some serious concern about the impact of this expenditure of resources on the educational programs of higher education is in order. Abetted by a federal bureaucracy, the intrusion could be great.

That these concerns are not chimerical is shown by the case of Marie E. Wirsing, who challenged the use of an assessment that, in her view, improperly represented the scholarly intention of her courses. Professor Wirsing, a faculty member in the School of Education at the University of Colorado, Denver, ran afoul of the assessment policies of the university's board of regents in its attempt to satisfy a state law requiring compliance with a "higher education accountability program." In Colorado, a mandated procedure was established to evaluate faculty, which according to Wirsing, "automatically establishes a given normative attitude of educational practitioners; it universalizes a single standard of presumed correctness. The imposition of any single intellectual outlook and associated behavior raises grave questions relative to education in a democratic society" (1989, p. 21).

The issue is not whether to agree with the content of the specific questions or procedures used for evaluation. Wirsing characterizes them as illustrative of the "positivist-realist-behaviorist tendency to operationalize and mechanize the whole of the educational process" (p. 20). I certainly reject the anti-positivist approach to social science. The point is that such procedures offer a means of controlling and directing faculty, when employed by administrators to allocate resources and judge faculty members. Wirsing advocated, as part of her courses, evaluation based on "philosophical principles and historical factors"; she was thus put in the position of affirming the use of procedures with which she took intellectual exception. That should be a matter of concern to all faculty. Her efforts to find redress in the courts have not been successful. She appealed an adverse ruling from the Federal District Court to the Tenth Circuit Court of Appeals and eventually to the Supreme Court, to no avail. While one can argue that legal adjudication should not be the main source of protection for academic freedom, as has McDonald (1992), the tendency of the courts to react to Wirsing's petition in terms of employer-employee law is not entirely satisfactory. The results of her case argue strongly that nonjudicial remedies should be employed by faculty to deal with the almost certain undesirable academic consequences of the growing assessment movement.

Some urgency in this matter is suggested because the accrediting associations have begun to call for assessments as a condition of accreditation. A draft statement issued by the Southern Association of Colleges and Schools asserts that "all member institutions are expected to document quality by employing a comprehensive system of planning and assessment in all aspects of institutional life" (Rogers, quoted in Hogan, 1994). What this mandate might mean in practice remains to be seen, but administrative forays into the classroom seem likely.

Protecting Academic Freedom in the Classroom

It is difficult to identify the circumstances that lead to successful intrusions of external entities into academic settings. Internal compliance plays a part. The overstaffing of universities may create conditions where people, looking for tasks to occupy themselves or aggrandize their offices, welcome the monitoring and enforcement of rules and guidelines with little regard for their educational impact. Administrative bloat has been discussed elsewhere (Bergmann, 1991; Halfond, 1991; Andersen, 1991). It does seem to offer an impediment to dealing effectively with real educational problems.

If there is a fundamental lesson in these movements and their impact on higher education, it is that rigorous educational and scholarly goals must remain first in efforts to make things better. Other matters should always be secondary. Moreover, the faculty should have primary control over these goals, and they should have the authority to resist efforts to subvert them to any other purposes, however laudable they may be. Hostile atmospheres are not desirable in educational institutions. We should know what we are doing, what we are doing well, and what we are doing poorly. Yet efforts to avoid harassment or to assess our activities should never be allowed to direct or demean our educational goals. Well-intentioned but intellectually poorly informed people acting through bureaucratic structures to achieve high-sounding goals represent a serious challenge to academic freedom and to the educational goals such freedom is intended to support.

Accordingly, certain policies seem necessary for higher education. First, speech and activities in the classroom should be under the control of individual faculty members. While probationary faculty may be under some greater control from others, that control should be from other faculty members and should be minimal. Second, only charges of scholarly failure should be a basis for questioning classroom conduct, and that questioning should be in the hands of faculty, not affirmative action officers, representatives of religious groups, political leaders, student activists, or others who are unqualified to judge academic performance. Third, when members of the academic community break laws, society's legal institutions should deal with the problem. Finally, speech codes and assessment protocols should be eschewed by universities in favor of informal norms and procedures centered in institutional departments, which protect decorum and enforce excellence. Faculty members must individually and collectively, through their professional organizations, resist intrusive forces whenever they appear. Our vigilance, rather than court protection, may be the most effective means of ensuring freedom in the classroom.

References

Andersen, K. E. "Anatomizing Bloat." *Academe,* 1991, 77 (6), 20–24.
Angelo, T. "Assessing Classroom Assessments: What We Have Learned in Seven Years"

(audiotape). American Association for Higher Education, 8th Conference on Assessment in Higher Education, 1993. (Audiotape no. 93C AHE-41, Mobiltape Company, Inc., 25061 W. Ave., Suite 70, Valencia, Calif.)

Benjamin, E. "The Decline of Academic Autonomy in Higher Education." *Academe,* 1994, *80* (4), 34–36.

Bergmann, B. R. "Bloated Administration, Blighted Campuses." *Academe,* 1991, 77 (6), 12–16.

Coleman, J. C. "On the Self-Suppression of Academic Freedom." *Academic Questions,* 1990–91, *4* (1), 17–22.

Fitzgerald, L. F. "Sexual Harassment: The Definition and Measurement of a Construct." In M. A. Paludi (ed.), *Ivory Power.* Albany: State University of New York Press, 1987.

"Formal Procedures for Handling Complaints of Discriminatory Harassment." *Emory Report,* 1991, *44* (8), 5–6.

Gross, B. R. "The Case of Philippe Rushton." *Academic Questions,* 1989, *3* (4), 35–46.

Halfond, J. A. "How to Control Administrative Cost." *Academe,* 1991, 77 (6), 17–19.

Hogan, R., "Proposed Revision in Institutional Effectiveness Criteria" (Internet). Higher Education Processes Conference Hall (Heproc-L@American.Edu), 1994.

Honan, W. H. "Professor Ousted for Lecture Gets Job Back." *New York Times,* Sept. 17, 1994, p. 18.

Jacobs, L. A. "Political or Pedagogical Correctness." *Academic Questions,* 1993, 6 (2), 59–62.

Leonard, R., and others. "Sexual Harassment at North Carolina State University." In G. L. Kreps (ed.), *Sexual Harassment: Communication Implications.* Creskill, N.J.: Hampton Press, 1993.

Longanecker, D. A. "The New Federal Focus on Accreditation." *Academe,* 1994, *80* (4), 13–17.

McDonald, M. P. "A Lawyer's Brief Against Litigating Academic Disputes." *Academic Questions,* 1992, *5* (4), 9–18.

Salemi, J. S. "Political Correctness at Dallas Baptist University: The Firing of David Ayers and John Jeffrey." *Measure,* 1992, *108,* 1–13.

Thernstrom, S. "McCarthyism Then and Now." *Academic Questions,* 1990–91, *4* (1), 14–15.

Tobin, R. W. "The Age of Accreditation: A Regional Perspective." *Academe,* 1994, *80* (4), 26–33.

Warren, D. L. "Why Faculty Should Care About Federal Regulation of Higher Education." *Academe,* 1994, *80* (4), 18–19.

Wirsing, M. E. "Academic Freedom and Teaching Foundations of Higher Education: A Personal Memoir." *Educational Foundations,* Fall 1989, pp. 7–32.

WILLIAM W. PENDLETON is associate professor of sociology at Emory University.

Exploitation and harassment of students are not protected by academic freedom, but are best addressed by faculty assurance of ethical professional conduct rather than speech codes.

It's Power, Stupid!

Mary W. Gray

That rape is about violence and not about sex has become generally recognized. That sexual harassment of students by faculty is about power and not about academic freedom needs also to be understood. The appropriate regulation of harassment is not through speech codes that restrict academic freedom but rather through insistence that faculty members adhere to professional ethics. Faculty have an ethical obligation to abstain from abusing students, whatever the basis of the abuse ("Statement on Professional Ethics," 1990, p. 76); moreover, they have a responsibility to refrain from introducing irrelevant and inappropriate material into the classroom, again whatever its nature ("1940 Statement of Principles on Academic Freedom and Tenure," 1990, p. 3; "Statement of the Association's Council," 1990, p. 78).

That the abuse of students may be verbal and not physical does not convert it into conduct protected by academic freedom. Nor does academic freedom give one the right to devote time that should be spent teaching course subject matter to crude sexual jokes (nor for that matter to repeated lengthy discussions of the previous night's football game). It is true that judgment is involved in deciding what is appropriate subject matter and what is abuse and that judgments differ; ultimately, should the question of disciplining a faculty member arise, the determination of what is appropriate must be made by a faculty committee. The standard that such a committee might use should not only be that of whether a "reasonable" student would have found it difficult, if not impossible, to learn effectively under certain conditions, but also whether "reasonable" faculty members would have conducted themselves in such a manner as did the accused.

The focus in this essay is on such faculty-student interactions. Faculty conduct toward colleagues or staff, on the other hand, occurs in an employment setting and thus comes under the purview of Title VII of the Civil Rights Act of 1964. Judicial interpretations of this act deem sexual harassment to be prohibited as a form of sex discrimination; although it is possible to disagree with these interpretations, they are, in fact, the law. This law applies to the academic workplace as to any other, and it is nonproductive, as well as ill-advised, to argue that the academic enterprise requires an exemption. Moreover, although there are professional ethical considerations involved in one's relationship with colleagues and staff, harassment in the workplace as such does not touch the essence of the academic enterprise the way that conduct toward students does. Thus, "hostile environment" harassment is generally forbidden in the academy as it is in other workplaces.

In those areas, however, where academic freedom is essential to the faculty's scholarship and, especially, teaching of students, the protections of academic freedom should limit the scope of any prohibitions; within these confines it is professional ethics that must regulate faculty behavior. In other words, if a certain academic discourse is alleged to be harassing, the first question must be whether the discourse was professionally appropriate. Accordingly, harassment allegations stemming from academic discourse should be subject to professional peer review conducted in accordance with the procedures and standards generally appropriate to allegations of unprofessional conduct.

It might be argued that because the protections of academic freedom extend to speech and writing outside the classroom, how such discourse is perceived by coworkers should be subject to the same considerations, rather than the usual regulations covering the workplace. To a certain extent this is true—colleagues could certainly feel harassed by what is said in a colloquium talk, a department meeting, or in other venues where speech is protected by academic freedom. In such cases the same considerations apply as in the context of faculty-student interactions, except that the effect on a "reasonable" colleague rather than on a "reasonable" student must be considered.

This essay does not address the more volatile and complex issue of student-to-student harassment. However, the responsibility of faculty members to maintain an appropriate classroom atmosphere is clear. Students are not bound by the same standards of professional ethics as are instructors, but perhaps they should be. We deal with other ethical infractions on the part of students through an honor code—why not deal with harassment in the same way? How about "I will not lie, cheat, steal, or harass my fellow students, nor others in the university community"?

Sexual Harassment

What then of sexual harassment by a professor, in or out of the classroom? Insofar as harassment involves conduct, the rules are not unlike those that cover the workplace. For example, unwanted contact is out-of-bounds, but "unwanted" needs to be interpreted in the faculty-student context—"consent" given within a power relationship is not truly consent. It has been said that in

England professors think they are god, and in Germany they are god. Even though professors in the United States generally do not claim godlike powers, unfortunately many have seen sexual relationships with students as a fringe benefit of their profession.

Some issues are easy—no threats, physical or verbal; no quid pro quo offers of good grades or other preferment in exchange for sexual favors; and clearly no retaliation for favors not granted, even if there was no quid pro quo in the asking. To assert that one has First Amendment or academic freedom rights to tell a student that the student's success in a course depends on engaging in sexual relations or even in agreeing to have dinner is simply absurd. Unwanted physical contact is as inappropriate in a faculty-student relationship as it is in an employer-employee context. Moreover, it is important to keep in mind, in deciding what constitutes sex harassment, that sexual harassment is considered to be sexual discrimination. Among other things, it is not the case that sex discrimination must have a single targeted victim; sex discrimination can well be directed at an entire group of victims, whether by deciding to pay women $1,000 less than men or by consistently refusing to call on women in class.

One form of sexual harassment that is all too prevalent on campuses is the harassment of gays and lesbians. Although the legal protections may be different, depending on local law, the ethical considerations are the same—namely, academic freedom is constrained by the obligations of the profession.

One could attempt to make a detailed list of forbidden actions, but the ingenuity of a harasser would likely circumvent such a catalogue of prohibitions. The absence of an internal sense of propriety invites external codes of conduct, which are inevitably both intrusive and ineffective. Therefore we must rely upon the faculty's professional judgement to distinguish which actions are appropriate and which are not. Nevertheless, some examples can be a helpful guide for building on the tried-and-true methods of case law to establish some parameters:

Dating students. Asking a student for a date is inappropriate when the student is subject to the control of the faculty member—if the student is in the faculty member's class, has the faculty member as a dissertation adviser, and so on. It is a question of power, not of personal freedom or romance. If it is real romance, it will wait until the power relation no longer exists. The press has reported that a group is being formed to champion the rights of faculty members to have "consensual" relations with their students. The answer to this is basically that there is no such thing in the professor-student setting.

Personal comments. Personal comments that make a student uncomfortable are inappropriate; however, there really is a threshold here based on a "reasonable student" standard. For example, "that tight sweater really makes you look sexy" is out of line, but "that's a nice sweater" may not be. However, as with workplace conduct, persistence is a consideration. Constant repetition of seemingly innocuous remarks that are causing discomfort is simply inappropriate. Academic freedom is not intended to apply to personal comments to students. Although First Amendment protection may well extend to such comments if the state acts to forbid them, such speech is nonetheless professionally unacceptable.

General comments. Classroom comments that make for a hostile atmosphere are unethical unless there is some pedagogical reason for them. For example, the assertion that there have been few great women mathematicians may be discomforting to women students in a mathematics class, but it is a statement that is entirely appropriate in introducing a discussion of what the reasons are for this scarcity. On the other hand, the statement "women can't do math" would be hard to justify, except as a discussion provoker. Even then, persistent repetition may rise to the level of harassment.

Clearly, stating that an individual woman will never succeed in mathematics solely because she is a woman is impermissible. Again, this is a question of power. Nearly every woman mathematician has been subject to similar comments and has survived, but when the source of the remark is someone who has the power to affect whether or not she *will* succeed, it must be taken much more seriously. Moreover, who knows how many women are *not* mathematicians largely because of such discouragement. Such comments are simply unprofessional. No student should be subjected to them, even in a sanitized form, much less when they are formulated as "You must be good in bed because you certainly aren't good at the board."

Explicit comments. This leads to comments of a sexual nature. Here again, professional judgment and a "reasonable student" standard must be applied. We also need some recognition of degrees of culpability. If accurate, reports of the suspension and requirement to undergo counseling of a professor who compared writing to intercourse seem like overkill. Moreover, such situations trivialize the whole issue of sexual harassment.

I like the statement on sexual harassment adopted by the Association for Women in Mathematics, so long as we keep in mind that certain speech enjoys the protection of academic freedom (*Newsletter of the Association for Women in Mathematics,* 1993, p. 15):

1. Sexual harassment is extremely serious. Sexual harassment, no matter how it may appear to the perpetrator, is ultimately about power, not sex. It is demoralizing and destructive for the victim. Sexual harassment has grave consequences for our profession, contributing to loss of talent and alienation of women from mathematical professions.
2. Sexual harassment has many forms. Sexual harassment is *the intrusion of sexuality into inappropriate contexts.* Sexual harassment has many forms besides seduction: words, gestures, body language, office decorations (the nude calendar), jokes . . . even where people focus their eyes (e.g., on breasts instead of faces).
3. Sexual harassment must be taken seriously. Institutions should put people on notice of the seriousness of the issue and of appropriate procedures to fol-

low in reporting violations of policy. Faculty, staff and student handbooks should cover these points, which should also be covered in other effective information dissemination (e.g., new faculty and student orientations).
4. Sexual harassment must be dealt with promptly. Once charges are made of sexual harassment, they should be dealt with as quickly as is feasible, for the sake of the accuser, the accused, and especially the wider community. Delay in dealing with sexual harassment charges leads to a loss of trust in the institution's goodwill.
5. Sexual harassment charges must be dealt with fairly. Procedures for dealing with sexual harassment should be not only quick but fair. They should be established with input from all segments of the institution, and peers should be involved in the judgment of peers (faculty members with faculty; students with students, etc.).
6. Sexual harassment charges must be dealt with compassionately. Staff members who are expected to be the first to deal with harassment charges should be trained to be sensitive to the issue. Although long delays in reporting may adversely affect the ability to get effective redress, procedures need to provide for the reality that victims are not always able, for psychological or professional reasons, to come forward quickly. The institution's sexual harassment policy should encourage victims to come forward in a timely fashion, but should set no time limits in which charges should be brought.
7. Sexual harassment must be dealt with effectively. Because of confidentiality, sexual harassment is often essentially not dealt with at all—a letter in a confidential file and a promise of changed behavior is simply not enough. Real consequences, such as loss of salary or termination of certain duties, may unwittingly be prematurely canceled by new administrations. The consequences of sexual harassment should be real and should be backed up by systematized institutional memory.
8. Sexual harassment must not be tolerated. At every large institution (and many small ones) there are those about whom reports of sexual harassment have circulated, but who have never been subjected to institutional inquiry and/or action. Supervisors need to be as concerned as they would be if the issue were bad teaching or plagiarism and need to take an active stance where this seems justified, in fairness to all concerned.

Sometimes it is argued in sex-discrimination cases that expressed views are irrelevant if they are not acted upon. "Yes," a department chair will relate, "I did say repeatedly at departmental meetings that I thought women with small children should stay at home and take care of them, but that did not influence my recommendation against tenure for Professor X, the mother of two children under five." Judges and juries have a hard time believing in such academic detachment. If what the chair says is true, he may not be guilty of sex discrimination, but he is certainly guilty of a breach of professional ethics, a breach we would not expect from a "reasonable" professor. Nor would we expect the work of a "reasonable" colleague in this chair's department to be unaffected by the persistent expression of such views. Most probably, were her credentials comparable to those of a male who was granted tenure, even a single utterance of this sort would be considered evidence of sex discrimination.

In the classroom the standards for a "pure" harassment case might be different. It is unlikely that a single such statement would be found to constitute harassment; and in fact, if appropriate to the subject matter under discussion, it might be protected by academic freedom. That is, a sociology professor teaching a course on marriage and the family might present evidence and arguments supporting the assertion that single mothers of small children should stay home. Claims that such a professionally relevant, if controversial, presentation in such a class caused tension or lack of sleep or made working or studying more difficult do not make a case that the presentation constitutes harassment. But if such a statement were totally irrelevant to the subject matter of the class, it could constitute a breach of professional ethics. And if a student who had small children could show that her grade in that professor's class was less than she deserved, again the evidence of sex discrimination would be strong.

Thus, prohibitions on speech that arise from professional ethical considerations are both broader and narrower than legal prohibitions against sexual harassment. Some statements protected by the First Amendment are, nonetheless, unprofessional and unprotected by academic freedom. On the other hand, some statements that cause discomfort and feel harassing are professionally appropriate and protected. In domains protected by academic freedom, it is academic freedom that must prevail.

Academic Freedom

What then *can* faculty profess? Certainly they can profess many ideas that may not be popular with students; indeed, they can profess ideas that may make some students uneasy or uncomfortable. Challenging students with ideas or interpretations that are new or even unwelcome to them is a part of education. On the other hand, faculty have a professional obligation not to introduce inappropriate material into the classroom. The question of the intrusion of faculty members' personal opinions arises not only in the case of sexual harassment but, for example, in the recent case of a professor disciplined for allowing his religious views to intrude into his teaching of physical education (*Bishop* v. *Aronov et al., 1991*).

Although faculty members are professionally obliged not to teach as fact that which is opinion (this is the basis of the creationism controversy) or even worse that which is false, there are occasions when such material is put before the class for purposes of provoking discussion and challenging the class. Instructors must make the decision as to the appropriateness of such material to the subject matter they teach and the pedagogy they use. However, it is necessary to recognize that there are abuses. Many of these may be resolved informally by advice and counsel. One of my first tasks as department chair years ago was to deal with a faculty member who felt it appropriate in a programming course to compare the size of the classroom chalk to that of the penises of various persons.

When there is a formal charge regarding a teacher's conduct, the faculty member is entitled to due process, in particular to have the case heard by other faculty. Unfortunately, on many campuses any allegation of harassment takes student complaints out of normal channels into a summary administrative process or a hearing by a group with little, if any, faculty participation. This is inappropriate because, as discussed above, the assurance of academic freedom requires consideration of whether the conduct was consistent with professional behavior. This finding depends initially on peer judgment. This does not mean, however, that faculty have the final word regarding faculty conduct. Generally accepted standards for the review of faculty conduct assign final authority for disciplinary sanctions to the governing board of the institution or to an independent arbitrator ("Recommended Institutional Regulations," 1990, p. 27; "Arbitration in Cases of Dismissal," 1990, pp. 65–68).

To decide what is relevant is never easy; examples used to illustrate course content—although such examples may be entirely appropriate to the subject matter—may easily be slanted in such a way that students might feel harassed, sexually or in other ways. For example, I teach a course in statistical methodology for graduate students in the social and natural sciences. I happened to notice that the text I was using had what seemed to be an unusual number of examples dealing with survey results on the death penalty; the examples generally showed (reflecting reality) that a majority of those surveyed favor capital punishment. However, there were always breakdowns showing that pro-death penalty views were far more prevalent among less well educated, blue-collar workers and those classified as having "conservative" Protestant religious views. Again, this reflects reality. I am strongly anti-death penalty, but I began to wonder how this would look to students who were not.

Closer examination of the textbook made it clear that it probably could be used as evidence of the "liberal" bias that conservatives assert permeates higher education. There were results showing that children of working mothers do better in school than children of mothers who do not work outside the home, results showing that depth of religious feeling is negatively correlated with income, results showing that anti-abortion sentiment is negatively correlated with education. Of course, I suppose that one would consider these results to indicate a liberal bias only if one subscribes to the theory that the more income and the more education, the better. However, the bottom line is the question of whether there is anything objectionable about the use of this text, given that the statistics are correct.

The example is not frivolous. About a dozen years ago a text for a basic mathematics course used IQ and bust size as an example of negative correlation. Complaints to the author from a number of faculty around the country were ignored. However, it turns out that large-enrollment basic mathematics classes are disproportionately under the control of women faculty; soon sales of this text fell dramatically. The next edition omitted the example. (It should be noted that the example did not pretend to relate real statistics.)

At the time I was delighted, for it seemed a good way to deal with restraints on speech—don't read what you don't want to read. But suppose every example likely to upset a particular constituency were to be removed from a textbook. Statistics texts would be pretty dull. (Yes, I know lots of people think they are already.) I'm still for registering complaints; the author simply has to make a professional judgment as to the appropriateness of an example and its contribution to the liveliness and interest of the text versus its potential for offense. However, I would be opposed to disciplining a faculty member for writing a text, no matter how offensive.

It is true, as some feminists and others argue, that the United States' devotion to the primacy of the First Amendment is virtually unique. For example, although many think of the Hyde Park Corner soapbox as a model for free speech, the United Kingdom has no constitutional nor statutory free speech guarantee other than as regards labor disputes. (Of course, it has no written constitution at all.) Canada makes it a crime to deny that the Holocaust occurred. Many other countries forbid "hate" speech—generally defined to include any statement taken to demean a particular racial or ethnic group. Similarly, the Universal Declaration of Human Rights proclaims the right to be free from hate speech. Amnesty International, the international human rights organization, has grappled for many years with the question of whether someone imprisoned for violating such hate speech laws should be adopted as a prisoner of conscience—that is, someone imprisoned for the peaceful expression of an opinion.

Nonetheless, the primacy the United States accords to free speech in general, and academic freedom in particular, is appropriate and necessary. What feminists against pornography seem to ignore is that if the First Amendment were a less well regarded principle, much of what feminists want to be available might not be—such as birth control information. In fact, even with the pervasive primacy of free speech considerations, these considerations lost out in the courts when balanced against the right of the federal government to forbid the dissemination of information about abortion in federally funded facilities.

In order to avoid constraints on academic speech, it would be well to have the phrase "hostile environment" retired as applied to academic interactions. Students (and colleagues, for that matter) cannot—if they are to learn—avoid hearing things they would rather not hear. The study of subject matter that may offend some students or colleagues does not constitute a hostile environment, but because it may be embarrassing and discomfiting, it has too often been confused with one. This confusion trivializes the very real problem of sexual harassment. In fact, the excessive focus on such examples almost seems a deliberate attempt to distract attention from a serious and continuing problem.

Academic Freedom Without Sexual Harassment

Faculty members do have an obligation not only to avoid harassment and discrimination but also to take positive action to provide an atmosphere for learning and for full realization of students' potential. To address this obligation we need to

Eliminate threats or other abuse of power in personal relationships
Eliminate quid pro quo speech
Eliminate unwanted touching or other physical harassment (for example, "stalking" or persistent phone calls)
Eliminate discrimination on the basis of sex, sexual orientation, or other factors unrelated to performance
Hold professors responsible for ethical conduct, including restricting their classroom speech to what is appropriate to the subject matter and otherwise providing an atmosphere conducive to learning
Act promptly, appropriately, fairly, and decisively when improper conduct occurs.

Those who want to be seen simultaneously to oppose sexual harassment and to defend academic freedom have tried to make a distinction between "targeted" and "untargeted" speech, limiting harassment allegations to the former ("Academic Freedom and Sexual Harassment," 1994, p. 72). This is a distinction without a difference—such facially reasonable parsing of the issue is doomed to failure because it is neither an adequate response to harassment nor an adequate protection of free speech. One need only consult those who have been the subject of "untargeted" harassment to understand this.

For example, for a professor to make repeated assertions in class that women are inferior—whether it be in their inability to do first-rate mathematics, art, philosophy, or whatever or simply their general lack of intelligence or diligence—constitutes sexual harassment, regardless of whether the remarks are directed to a specific woman in the class or to women in general. (As discussed above, such remarks would be protected if discussion of gender differences was integral to the specific course and if the manner of argument was professionally appropriate.) Yes, such remarks *do* create a hostile atmosphere, one that is more debilitating for some women than for others. Are we to expect each woman to make the situation less hostile for herself by public disagreement? But more relevant than "atmosphere" is the fact that the teacher-student relationship is one of power, and this is an abuse of it. To suggest that the only appropriate remedy is "more speech" is simply absurd.

Nonetheless, such harassment should not be forbidden by means of a speech code, for to restrict speech is not the function of a university. What should happen is that the professor should be called to account for unethical behavior. Those harassed must have a means to make their complaints known, and the accused professor must have access to due process. It is not enough to say that it is a tough world, that we cannot be overly protective, or to make similar excuses. It is the responsibility of the profession to enforce ethical standards—but as adherence to professional standards, not as suppression of academic freedom.

Whenever the 1992 Clinton campaign appeared to be floundering in a maze of complicated issues, conflicting policies, and voter discontent, the rallying cry was "It's the economy, stupid!" With this reminder the campaign's focus returned to the winning issue, the center of concern for the majority of Americans, the putative cause of all the country's problems, and the salvation not only of the campaign but of the ills of society.

The current campus controversy over sexual harassment has a similarly simple focus—power. In particular, faculty members have a professional responsibility that precludes their using power to harass students and colleagues. This ethical responsibility is not overridden by any First Amendment or academic freedom rights. It is not that freedom to swing one's arm ends where another's nose begins; it is that freedom of speech ends where it is inconsistent with professional ethics.

It is my belief that the furor over the excesses of the policing of sexual harassment comes from those who resist any oversight of their conduct toward students or colleagues. Those who persist in unethical behavior—be it harassment, other discrimination, plagiarism, scientific misconduct, or other transgressions—cannot hide behind academic freedom.

Justice Potter Stewart was known for declaring that he knew pornography when he saw it. I do not claim an analogous prescience for sexual harassment. What I do claim is that academic freedom cannot protect sexual harassment, nor is academic freedom undermined by the policing of sexual harassment; for sexual harassment presupposes unprofessional behavior, behavior that is not entitled to the protections of academic freedom. Faculty have an ethical obligation not to engage in harassment and an ethical responsibility to hold colleagues accountable if they do so.

References

"Academic Freedom and Sexual Harassment." *Academe,* Sept.–Oct. 1994, p. 72.
"Arbitration in Cases of Dismissal." In *AAUP Policy Documents and Reports.* Washington, D.C.: American Association of University Professors, 1990, pp. 65–68.
Bishop v. Aronov et al. [926 F. 2d 1066 (11th Cir. 1991)].
Newsletter of the Association for Women in Mathematics, Nov.–Dec. 1993, 23 (6), p. 15.
"1940 Statement of Principles on Academic Freedom and Tenure." In *AAUP Policy Documents and Reports.* Washington, D.C.: American Association of University Professors, 1990, pp. 3–10.
"Recommended Institutional Regulations." In *AAUP Policy Documents and Reports.* Washington, D.C.: American Association of University Professors, 1990, pp. 21–30.
"Statement of the Association's Council: Freedom and Responsibility." In *AAUP Policy Documents and Reports.* Washington, D.C.: American Association of University Professors, 1990, pp. 77–78.
"Statement on Professional Ethics." In *AAUP Policy Documents and Reports.* Washington, D.C.: American Association of University Professors, 1990, pp. 75–76.

MARY W. GRAY is *professor of mathematics at American University. She is an attorney and served for many years as chair of the Association of American University Professors' Committee on the Status of Women and as a member of its Committee A on Academic Freedom and Tenure.*

Corporate power and state action may diminish academic freedom, and, consequently, discourage beneficial research.

Fischer v. The Medical College of Georgia and the R.J. Reynolds Tobacco Company: A Case Study of Constraints on Research

Paul M. Fischer

On December 11, 1991, the *Journal of the American Medical Association* published the results of a small study I participated in, which indicated that children as young as three years of age were able to recognize cigarette brand logos and that Old Joe, the Camel cartoon character, was as recognizable by six-year-olds as Mickey Mouse on the Disney Channel logo. I knew at the time that the study would have important implications for public health and public policy. I did not know then that subsequent events would serve to demonstrate unfortunate changes that have taken place in the nature of American universities and their relationship to the political and corporate world. The story is a marker of the erosion of one university's responsibilities to its faculty, to the academic process, and to the pursuit of new knowledge.

Chronology of Events

December 11, 1991. Our study, as well as two others demonstrating the influence of cigarette advertising on teenagers, is released with great fanfare by the

---

Editors' note: This chapter consists primarily of the author's account of his own experience after publishing research findings concerning cigarette advertising and children. At his suggestion, we append selections from an American Association of University Professors affidavit on the case.

American Medical Association. A national press conference is held in New York to present the findings. The studies receive wide coverage in the press, including a five-minute "American Agenda" segment on the *ABC Nightly News.*

March 9, 1992. The American Medical Association, the surgeon general, the American Cancer Society, the American Heart Association, and the American Lung Association all call for a ban on Old Joe and restriction of cigarette advertising that is attractive to children. U.S. Surgeon General Antonio Novello says, "In the past, R.J. Reynolds would have us walk a mile for a Camel. Today it's time that we invite Old Joe himself to take a hike. . . . It's time for the tobacco industry to stop preying on our nation's youth."

March 10, 1992. James Johnson, CEO of the R.J. Reynolds Tobacco Company, defends Old Joe in an interview in *USA Today.* In this interview he misstates facts about the *JAMA* studies. He says the ". . . studies are flawed in very serious ways. The scientists who wrote these studies are not unbiased." Specifically, he states that the sample size of the study was 23, while in reality it was 229. He also claims that the children's parents were called the night before the study and asked only about cigarettes. No such cueing of parents occurred.

March 27, 1992. I am paged to the police office of the Medical College of Georgia (MCG) campus and am served a "Notice of Out-of-State Deposition on Oral Examination and Request for Production of Documents and Things" by the R.J. Reynolds Tobacco Company. A suit has been filed in California by Janet Mangini (a private citizen) against R.J. Reynolds, based on their failure to place health warnings on promotional products such as caps and T-shirts. The Mangini suit does not name my research; however, other studies in *JAMA* are cited. In the subpoena I am ordered by R.J. Reynolds to produce the following items relating to the *JAMA* study: the names and telephone numbers of all the children that participated in the study; all drafts of the study design; all notes, memos, and videotapes pertaining to the study; the names, addresses, telephone numbers, background information, and occupations of all interviewers; hard-copy tabulations and data tapes; originals of all test materials; all correspondence relating to the research; the names and addresses and background information for all consultants; the names and addresses of all funding sources; and the names and telephone numbers of all respondents who were excluded from the study.

My initial reaction is that the demand is ridiculous: R.J. Reynolds has no right to subpoena these records, since they are irrelevant to the subject of the California lawsuit. In addition, I have signed confidentiality agreements with each of the children's parents, promising that their identities would be treated with strict confidentiality. I naively assume that the university has the responsibility to protect me from this type of harassment because of their role in ensuring "academic freedom." I immediately contact Carol Huston, MCG legal adviser. She informs me that I have no legal options. I must appear on the stated date for deposition and must present all the materials requested in the subpoena. I immediately contact my own lawyer, Robert W. Hunter, III, who prepares a motion to quash the RJR subpoena.

April 6, 1992. A letter from Carol Huston to the state's Department of Law in Atlanta indicates the school's understanding that there is more at stake here than an innocent request by a company for research data:

> Dr. Fischer strongly desires for the subpoena to be quashed, or at least that the names of respondents and interviewers be protected, so as to prevent tobacco companies from intimidating researchers and people who participate in research studies. His concern, which I believe is well founded, is that Reynolds is attempting to harass him (and other researchers) through tactics such as this in order to discourage future research, the results of which may not be favorable to the tobacco industry. . . . We also believe if R.J. Reynolds obtains the names of the respondents, it seems very likely that Reynolds may contact them and attempt to harass them. This, in turn, may discourage other individuals from participating in future research projects. . . . We also believe it is important to attempt to protect the names of the persons who conducted the interviews, for reasons similar to those mentioned above. Should the interviewers be harassed by Reynolds, this may very well discourage other people from agreeing to serve as interviewers for fear that they will be drawn into litigation or be subject to other harassment.

April 23, 1992. The attorney general for the State of Georgia, the official counsel for the medical school, takes the position that the requested records belong to the school and are subject to the Georgia Open Records Act, a law designed to permit public access to *official records.* It should be noted that R.J. Reynolds has not requested the records through the Open Record Act; however, the attorney general's office considers the act to be the only law relevant to its position. In a letter from senior assistant attorney general, Kathryn L. Allen, to my lawyer, the attorney general's office states, "We have considered the matter being taken up by the Richmond Superior Court in the above case and decided this office cannot make an appearance. The Medical College of Georgia stated that in their view the subpoenaed records belong to it. Given that position, we believe that the records may well be subject to the Open Records Act request and we cannot take a position inconsistent with that act."

April 24, 1992. Chief Superior Court Judge William M. Flemming, Jr., of the Richmond Superior Court, State of Georgia, rules in favor of our motion to quash the RJR subpoena. RJR immediately appeals the ruling to the State Court of Appeals.

April 27, 1992. Advertising Age, a widely read advertising journal, reports the results of their own study to verify the *JAMA* findings. In this study of children ages eight to eighteen, the most familiar cigarette brand named was Camel (90 percent). When asked to circle items seen in cigarette ads, Camels were the top choice (picked by 94 percent). The study's author, Marion Salzman, president of BKG Youth, says, "I was blown away by the number of smaller kids who could name cigarettes" (Levin, 1992, p. 12).

June 19, 1992. An article in *Science* ("Who Controls the Researcher's Files?,"

1992) reports on RJR's legal actions against the *JAMA* authors. Joseph DiFranza, who studied the influence of Camel advertising on teenagers, turned over all of his research records to RJR. Some of these records were subsequently leaked to a reporter at RJR's hometown newspaper, the *Winston-Salem Journal*. An article in this newspaper implies scientific misconduct by Dr. DiFranza because he had indicated in correspondence prior to conducting the study his belief that cigarette advertising influenced teenagers. In the *Science* article, Peggy Carter, an R.J. Reynolds spokesman, confirms that the company intends to obtain the subjects' names for all of the *JAMA* studies through subpoena and then to call the children's homes to verify their participation. Her reason for this is that "[t]here have been a number of stories that have come up in recent years where scientists claimed to have produced research that . . . was never done at all" (p. 1621).

August 27, 1992. I believe that MCG's position regarding the release of the children's names is unethical, is not required under the Georgia Open Records Act, and is in violation of the school's agreements with the National Institute of Health (NIH) regarding research on human subjects. However, in a letter to the MCG dean (Gregory L. Eastwood), the school's senior legal adviser (Clayton D. Steadman) argues that the names should be turned over because "the research in question is not supported by federal funding, [so] no federal laws or regulations regarding research involving humans subjects would apply."

September 8, 1992. I am contacted by J. Thomas Puglisi, acting chief of the Compliance Oversight Branch, Office of Protection from Research Risks (OPRR) of the NIH. He has heard of the school's position regarding research subject confidentiality and asks my permission to use my name in contacting MCG regarding a potential breach of human subject protection. I agree.

September 14, 1992. Dr. Francis J. Tedesco, president of MCG, receives a letter from Thomas Puglisi regarding allegations of noncompliance by MCG in protecting human research subjects. The letter indicates that MCG, through its federal contract with the Department of Health and Human Services (DHHS), has agreed to meet all federal research regulations *without regard to source of funding*. The letter indicates that MCG's failure to ensure compliance with the human subjects regulation would put the institution in jeopardy of both existing and future DHHS support for research.

September 17, 1992. I speak with Don Wagner, executive secretary of the Georgia Conference of the American Association of University Professors (AAUP). He indicates that in addition to a human subjects violation, the school's position is in violation of university responsibilities in regard to academic freedom. He volunteers AAUP support.

September 22, 1992. I speak with Tom Puglisi about MCG's response to his letter. He says that while the institution does have a contract with the NIH which says that both federally and non-federally funded research will follow HHS human subjects regulations, all MCG needs to do is to renegotiate their DHHS contract so that it pertains only to federally funded research. The NIH general counsel has advised Dr. Puglisi that the NIH will limit its response to requiring renegotiation of the MCG contract. When I ask him about the reasons for this limited response he says, "Well, it's not really political, but how should I state this, in my discussion with the (NIH) general counsel it looks like that is all we will be able to do."

September 22, 1992. I am called to a meeting with the MCG president, medical school dean, vice president for research, my chairman, and two MCG lawyers. I ask that my lawyer be allowed to attend the meeting, but this request is denied. I ask that a faculty representative of my choice be allowed to attend. This too is denied. The administration is furious about the NIH inquiry. I ask how the school could accept a position of releasing the children's names when it entered into a legal contract with the parents through signed consent forms assuring them of confidentiality and anonymity. I note that the parents could sue the school if the names are released. Gerald Woods, the school's senior attorney, states that the school is ready to accept this possibility because they believe that any financial damages that might be imposed in such a suit would be quite small.

September 30, 1992. We travel to Atlanta for the hearing before the Court of Appeals. In his remarks, the RJR lawyer indicates that the records are obviously not accessible through the Open Records Act, since the research was not done with state support. The Appeals Court judges appear to be persuaded that my research is irrelevant to the original California lawsuit and that since I am neither an expert for Mangini nor R.J. Reynolds, my deposition is irrelevant.

October 7, 1992. MCG president Francis Tedesco responds to the NIH inquiry. In his response he indicates that the allegations are a "hypothetical question," since the school has not released any records. He does, however, indicate that if an Open Records request were made, "We would be compelled to disclose that information including the identities of research subjects." He reiterates that my research was not federally funded and that MCG will choose to follow their interpretation of the Open Records Act rather than their agreement with DHHS, should that choice have to be made. "The Medical College of Georgia's only formal obligation to protect confidentiality of research subjects is a voluntary obligation set forth in our assurance to the extent it is not in conflict with federal, state or local laws."

December 15, 1992. The MCG faculty senate unanimously adopts the following resolution:

> Whereas the research records of Paul M. Fischer, M.D., have been subpoenaed in a court case by the R.J. Reynolds Company, and
> Whereas these records include the names of children who participated in the study, and
> Whereas study participants were guaranteed anonymity by the study's informed consent document, approved by the Human Assurances Committee of the Medical College of Georgia,
> Therefore the faculty of the School of Medicine of the Medical College fully supports the legal efforts of Dr. Fischer to resist the release of this information, in the firm belief that it would be morally and ethically inappropriate to do so.

February 2, 1993. Francis J. Tedesco, president of MCG, receives a letter from Thomas Puglisi at the NIH accepting the renegotiated contract with HHS. The letter states, "[The NIH] recognizes that it lacks jurisdiction with respect to Dr. Fischer's research. Nevertheless, OPRR finds it lamentable that the Medical College of Georgia is unable to afford optimal confidentiality protection to the subjects who participated in this research and to subjects participating in other research that is not federally supported. Ethical standards clearly dictate that every effort be made to protect the confidentiality of identifiable private information obtained in research. Violations of this principle are particularly egregious in situations, such as Dr. Fischer's, which involve children or members of other potentially vulnerable groups."

February 9, 1993. The Court of Appeals rules in our favor, arguing that the documents sought are beyond the bounds of responsible discovery. The decision to quash the RJR subpoena is upheld. Dr. Tedesco calls to congratulate me on this successful action.

February 27, 1993. In an article in the *Augusta Chronicle* about my legal expenses, MCG lawyer Clay Steadman states that the school had not been involved in support of my legal efforts because of their position on the Open Records Act: "We decline to object to release of this information on the basis that although it was not an Open Records request, Open Records would have required us to release it." This position had been previously unknown to RJR, who had in fact indicated that they believed the information was *not* accessible under the Open Records Act.

March 4, 1993. As a result of the *Augusta Chronicle* article, James R. Johnson, legal counsel for R.J. Reynolds, sends a letter to H. Dean Propst, chancellor of the University System of Georgia, requesting my research records. The chancellor's office responds that the records are not on file in that office. (*Editors' note:* The University System of Georgia consists of Georgia's thirty-four public colleges and universities, including MCG. The system is governed by a single board, the Board of Regents, whose chief administrative officer is the chancellor.)

March 10, 1993. James R. Johnson submits an Open Records request for records related to the *JAMA* study. I am given forty-eight hours to turn over all requested records.

March 11, 1993. I meet with my chairman, Joseph Tollison, to see about complying with the school's request. I propose to turn the records over to the school if the school will initiate a review of the research to avoid any subsequent innuendo of scientific impropriety. (Dr. DiFranza was subjected to such accusations by his institution, the University of Massachusetts, after complaints were initiated to the university by RJR). Francis Tedesco, president of MCG, refuses to meet with me or my chairman. His legal counsel, Clay Steadman, indicates that I will be suspended if I do not turn over the documents. Tedesco tells my research colleague (Adam Goldstein) that the attorney general will have me arrested if I do not comply with the school's request.

March 12, 1993. Having been left with few options, and at the advice of my lawyer, I choose to turn all of the documents over to the court for protection until such time as the legal issues relating to the Open Records Act, academic freedom, and subject confidentiality can be clarified. The court approves a temporary restraining order against the Open Records request.

March 18, 1993. An editorial in the *Augusta Chronicle* titled "Blowing Smoke?" by Phillip A. Kent, editorial page editor, refers to my legal fight as "bizarre" (Kent, 1993, p. 4). I was not contacted by Mr. Kent, who erred in the editorial by stating that the California lawsuit relied on my research, that MCG's officials had supported my earlier legal efforts, and that R.J. Reynolds had won in court. (They had in fact lost twice.) When I contacted Mr. Kent by phone, he indicated that the information for the editorial had been obtained from an interview with MCG president Francis Tedesco.

March 29, 1993. The attorney general's office, acting on behalf of MCG, asks the court to drop the temporary restraining order. The request is denied.

April 15, 1993. Georgia's Governor Miller signs a bill to amend the Open Records Act to exclude from Open Records release the names of research participants. The bill receives public support from the AAUP, the president of the University of Georgia, and the Board of Regents. (*Editors' note:* When the bill moved through the state legislature its most visible and outspoken opponent was the Georgia Press Association. Officials of the Press Association testified against the bill before both House and Senate committees. There was no evidence that tobacco interests had any interest in the legislation, but the Press Association saw the bill as a step back from open government. At a lengthy meeting in Georgia Lt. Governor Pierre Howard's office [he supported the bill] officials from the Board of Regents, the executive director of the Press Association, the legal counsel for the *Atlanta Constitution,* the editorial page editor of the *Atlanta Journal,* and both the executive secretary and the chairman of the Government Relations Committee of the Georgia Conference of AAUP argued over the merits and consequences of the bill. At the conclusion of the meeting the Press Association dropped its opposition.)

April 23, 1993. RJR asks the court to join the Medical College of Georgia and the attorney general against me in the lawsuit. Both the attorney general's office and the Medical College of Georgia support RJR's motion to intervene. The suit ironically puts a medical school and a tobacco company together against a faculty member.

April 29, 1993. Paul H. L. Walter, past president of AAUP, submits an affidavit brief to the court in support of our position (see the Afterword at the end of this chapter). The brief outlines the legal basis for academic freedom and its treatment as a First Amendment issue. Dr. Walter states, ". . . it is my judgment that permitting the Medical College of Georgia to turn over to R.J. Reynolds the materials requested would in this circumstance have a serious adverse impact on the future conduct of socially beneficial scholarly work."

August 12, 1993. We receive a nine-page letter listing all of the documents and data now requested by RJR through the Open Records Act. It states that they want *everything* relating to the study, regardless of when generated or by whom. RJR asks that subject names be redacted from submitted documents.

September 7, 1993. A meeting of the parties is held at the suggestion of the judge. I indicate that I would turn over the requested documents, with the exception of the reviewer comments from *JAMA* and unpublished data. (The latter is specifically mentioned as not subject to the Open Records Act). The RJR counsel appears agreeable to this compromise, but Kathryn Allen, representing the attorney general's office and MCG, states that the case sets a precedent and that the institution wants to prove that professors do not have the right to withhold this kind of information. She states that even if I come to an agreement with RJR, the school will continue to pursue the case because of legal precedent.

September 1993. MCG releases to RJR all of its own records about the study, including those stored in the grants office and the statistics division. A large number of unpublished data are turned over, including data on alcohol advertising that is planned for future publication. I am not contacted to review this information prior to its release.

December 1, 1993. I resign from the Medical College of Georgia and enter private practice in Augusta.

July 20, 1994. Judge John H. Ruffin, Jr., signs a request written by RJR to release all of the records held by the court. Before we are notified of this decision, the court releases the original records to RJR, making an appeal of this decision moot.

Conclusion

Obviously, it is unwise to generalize about the status of academic freedom nationwide from the unique and unusual events of this case alone. However, there are a number of lessons to be learned from my experience:

- There has always been a difficult balance between the ideal of the university as a protected community of learners (an "ivory tower") and the reality of the political and corporate environment in which the university exists. In this case, no attempt to balance these forces was made. Traditional academic values, such as research subject confidentiality and academic freedom, were not considered relevant by those establishing university policy.
- Given the external political and corporate forces that influence (or control) the university's administration, it must be the responsibility of the faculty to preserve and protect traditional academic values. When the faculty believes it is powerless, it *is* powerless.
- In the selection of the university's leaders, it must be the faculty's responsibility to be very clear about these individuals' understanding of and commitment to academic values.
- Courage is a quality of individuals, not of institutions.

Afterword

Editors' note: The following remarks are excerpts from a deposition regarding Dr. Fischer's case by Paul H. L. Walter, former president of the AAUP and current chairman of the board of the American Chemical Society, submitted on behalf of the AAUP on April 29, 1993. The deposition reviews similar cases and outlines the major issues involved.

1. I am submitting this affidavit in support of the efforts of Dr. Paul Fischer to prevent the Medical College of Georgia from turning over to the R.J. Reynolds Tobacco Company ("R.J. Reynolds") the research materials relating to Dr. Fischer's study on the effects of tobacco advertising. . . . As more fully described below, I believe that the release of those materials would have a deleterious impact on the conduct of academic research not only at the Medical College of Georgia but also throughout the country. . . .

13. The ability to conduct scholarly research freely is an activity which lies at the heart of higher education and falls within the First Amendment's protection of academic freedom. Research and teaching activities are closely linked components of scholarly activity in American higher education. Academic freedom includes the freedom to search for knowledge; therefore, it is as much an infringement on a scholar's academic freedom to constrain or limit the scholar's research activities as to limit his or her freedom in the classroom. I believe that compelled disclosure of Dr. Fischer's research data under the Georgia Open Records Act would violate his right to academic freedom.

14. AAUP . . . [has argued] for a qualified privilege protecting scholars and researchers from the obligation to comply with demands for research data absent demonstration of a compelling need for the data. . . . AAUP [has] collected information on situations in which attempts have been made to compel the disclosure of scholarly research. The following accounts come from materials in the files of AAUP.

15. The Kinsey Institute at Indiana University, which conducted a well-known study of human sexuality, received a request from the Federal Bureau of Investigation in the early 1950s for information about individuals who participated, on a confidential basis, in the study. The Institute had pledged to preserve the anonymity of research subjects and the confidentiality of research results, and accordingly announced its intention to destroy all its research records and "accept the consequences of such defiance" if the FBI subpoenaed documents in the Institute's possession. Ultimately the FBI did not persist.

16. Another episode of some notoriety occurred during the Vietnam War era. Shortly after excerpts from the Pentagon Papers appeared in the *New York Times* and the *Washington Post,* a Harvard University faculty member named Samuel Popkin was subpoenaed to appear before a Massachusetts grand jury investigating the unauthorized release of this classified study. Professor Popkin, who specialized in East Asian studies and had conducted many interviews with Vietnamese and American sources in connection with his scholarly writing on American war policy in Vietnam, refused to answer questions from the grand jury concerning the substance of his conversations with confidential sources. Professor Popkin was subsequently held in contempt of court and jailed for several days, an event that galvanized the academic community

and led to calls for recognition of a judicially-recognized testimonial privilege protecting the confidentiality of academic research. . . .

17. Professor Paul Bullock, an economist at the University of California, Los Angeles, conducted research for many years on the "street economy" of the ghetto, during which he nurtured relationships with the leaders of several youth gangs. The relationships were jeopardized when a local police department panel investigating alleged police cooperation in ghetto crime tried to force Professor Bullock to disclose the identities of his research subjects. He successfully resisted, asserting that his sources would never share confidences with him again to the serious detriment of his research.

18. In other instances, disclosure has been sought from faculty members studying jeep design defects, the carcinogenicity of diethylstilbestrol, toxic shock syndrome, smoking and exposure to asbestos, the involvement of drug addicts in crime, crimes committed by police, economics of electric companies and rape victims. The American Political Science Association reported 80 attempts to compel the production of scholarly works between 1966 and 1976, and since then, there have been numerous other instances. . . .

19. As those examples illustrate, research that becomes the target of third party disclosure demands often concerns issues of public health, product design, public safety, or questions in the social sciences. The pursuit of scholarly work in these areas is of obvious importance to the public in combating disease, enhancing safety, and generally improving conditions in society. Should third parties be permitted to intrude into these scholarly endeavors absent a demonstration of compelling need, the inevitable result will be to diminish researchers' willingness to undertake such projects. Moreover, if research materials become subject to compelled disclosure, time which the scholar would otherwise spend on productive research would be spent instead on the production of materials.

20. Demands for research involving data obtained on an express promise to the individual that it would remain confidential pose additional problems. If researchers cannot reasonably guarantee such confidentiality, subjects will inevitably be less willing to cooperate. Although a researcher might try to assure a reluctant individual that materials will be redacted and identifying information deleted before disclosure, the individual may well, nonetheless, conclude that a serious risk of a breach of confidentiality remains.

21. The academic community itself effectively tests the reliability of research findings and conclusions, and there is little role for the courts in this process. Through publication, a scholar submits his or her methods and reasoning to the scrutiny of those who are best equipped to analyze them—fellow scholars in the field. This happens on two levels.

22. The first level of scrutiny is the peer review process that occurs before an article is accepted. . . .

23. The second level of the review is the replication of the published study or experiment by the researcher's peers. . . .

24. The methods described directly above are the traditional means by which an

academic researcher's results are tested and verified in the scientific community. It is not generally the case in the scientific community that the raw data and other underlying documentation of a study are used by others to check the researcher's results. These traditional methods are presumably available to R.J. Reynolds.

25. In conclusion, it is my judgment that permitting the Medical College of Georgia to turn over to R.J. Reynolds the materials requested would in this circumstance have a serious adverse impact on the future conduct of socially beneficial scholarly work.

References

Kent, P. A. "Blowing Smoke?" *Augusta Chronicle,* Mar. 18, 1993, p. 4.
Levin, G. "Poll: Camel Ads Effective with Kids." *Advertising Age,* Apr. 27, 1982, p. 12.
"Who Controls the Researcher's Files?" *Science,* 1992, *256,* 1620–1621.

PAUL M. FISCHER *is a practicing physician and former professor in the Department of Family Medicine at the Medical College of Georgia. He is the editor of the* Journal of Family Practice.

Artistic expression merits protections of academic freedom similar to those accorded to intellectual expression.

Academic Freedom and Artistic Expression

Carol Simpson Stern

Academic freedom plays a major role in shaping how colleges and universities safeguard artistic expression. It protects the right of artists and teachers to create works and share them with larger publics through display, exhibition, and performance. What, if any, limitations should be imposed on artistic expression? Is it permissible for an artwork to be removed from its place of display, or for an instructor to be told to stop showing slides of nudes in an art history class, in response to complaints that the artist or teacher is racially insensitive or guilty of sexual harassment? Are there circumstances that justify the suppression of an artistic production? This essay examines some of these issues, drawing on actual examples and offering practical advice. It argues that great harm will result if we accord artistic creation, performance, and exhibition on campus less protection than is traditionally accorded the spoken and printed word. It urges faculty members and administrator to resist efforts to encroach on the art teacher's classroom presentations or course content.

Public Furor over Art and Artists

Teachers of the fine and performing arts at institutions of higher education are encountering numerous challenges to their right to independently teach artistic ideas and to create, produce, and display works of art on campuses. These challenges come from diverse groups whose appeals for censorship fly under different banners: diversity or multiculturalism, feminism, religion, good taste, and the public good.

In the past few years there has been a disturbing increase in the number of cases in which artistic works displayed on campuses have enraged publics and led to demands that the artwork be removed from its place of display. In one widely publicized case, students working through their student union governing board commissioned a painter to make a mural of Malcolm X for a plaza on the campus of San Francisco State University in front of the student union. The artist's representation of Malcolm X's face was framed by a border of Stars of David and skulls and crossbones, provoking a fierce display of outrage by many in the community and on campus who found the work flagrantly anti-Semitic and singularly inappropriate ("San Francisco State Destroys Malcolm X Mural After Furor," 1994).

After failing to resolve the issue by working with the student governing board, the president of the university ordered the mural to be sandblasted off the face of the public building on which it was displayed. The episode caused a storm of protest, crystallizing a number of important issues for educators to address: What, if any, are the rights of the artist to have his work displayed on a public building? What procedures should be followed in selecting art in such cases? What are the rights of the public not to have offensive works forced involuntarily on them in public spaces on campus? If the final artwork substantively departs from the rendering submitted for approval by the artist prior to entering into a contract, does the work constitute speech that is protected under either the First Amendment or academic freedom? What educational values should prevail when contesting groups assert seemingly irreconcilable positions? How can the cause of cultural diversity be advanced if one group is allowed to vilify another under the rubric of academic freedom?

Other cases raise related issues. A professor at Vanderbilt University is accused of sexual harassment by a former student ("A Conflict About Art," 1993). She accuses him of displaying photographs of nude human subjects, including one of himself and his wife, and discussing sexually explicit photography in a fine arts class. Most of the photographs were actually presented by students in the class, as a part of a class project. Although Vanderbilt declined to take formal disciplinary action against the professor, it did pursue an internal investigation of the issues. The result was that the professor was asked to provide all students in his class with a warning at the beginning of the semester. The warning was to include a description of the materials to be shown in class and a statement that students would be free to leave class without penalty if they were offended. Newspaper accounts of the events report that the Freedom Forum's First Amendment Center at Vanderbilt sponsored a forum, "Freedoms in Conflict," to publicly air the issues involved (Bostick, 1993; Parsons, 1993). One of the questions before the group was whether the professor committed sexual harassment or whether it was the classroom subject matter that caused the discomfort, and whether that particular subject matter was necessary to the course content. The dean was placed in the position of having to decide whether to discipline the professor for sexual harassment or whether to defend his actions as an unavoidable part of his academic duties as an instructor of art.

In the state of Iowa, the state legislature recently issued a requirement that professors of art provide very detailed syllabi that clearly announce their intention to display or discuss works that may offend. The creators of this legislation argue that it is a necessary protection of the consumer's right to know. They insist that students have a right to choose whether or not they wish to be subjected to pornographic images and nude bodies when they elect to take a class or visit a gallery or theatrical space on campus. The counterargument states that this kind of requirement, imposed only on arts educators and not scientists or others in the academic community, is a thinly disguised attempt to censor arts and chill its expression. In short, the opponents of this legislation believe it to be inimical to the spirit of creativity and intellectual discovery that the concept of academic freedom rightly protects.

In such an environment it is worth revisiting the subject of academic freedom. In particular, it is important to consider how academic freedom applies to the expressive arts, to artistic expression and display that is not precisely analogous to the spoken or printed word (the spheres educators are accustomed to protecting under the rubric of academic freedom). Many artworks are complete only once they've been "performed" before an audience, either in a class, a theater, or a gallery (that is, once they've been placed on exhibit). In short, art often moves from score or text into realization in a moment of enactment that requires an audience. It is this performative dimension of much art—a kind of rite of publication of sorts—that presents many of the most vexing problems when shaping a policy on academic freedom; such policies should be sensitive to the nuances of this particular brand of expression. In a climate in which feminists, multiculturalists, religionists, and others are clamoring for control and in which legislators and the public are intruding into the teaching process and seeking to regulate teaching tools (such as syllabi), it is even more necessary to reassert the prerogatives of academic freedom. When teachers of the arts lose the protections academic freedom affords, American universities are in danger of losing the foundation that has made them the envy of the world. Therefore it is critical to clarify what rights the arts teacher holds—and with these rights, what responsibilities.

Censorship and the Arts

Before considering current questions about artistic expression and academic freedom, it is useful to contextualize the current furor with a brief review of the history of censorship and the arts.

Censorship of art is not new. Many of the artworks we now consider to be great were banned in their own time. Michelangelo's Sistine Chapel frescoes depicted naked male genitalia, resulting in a call to cover the exposed parts. Degas's nudes, Picasso's ebullient, lusty, naked women, and Stravinsky's *Rite of Spring* were all banned from exhibition and concert halls. James Joyce's *Ulysses,* D.H. Lawrence's *Lady Chatterley's Lover,* and Henry Miller's *Tropic of Cancer* were banned as "obscene."

Robert M. O'Neil's essay "Artistic Freedom and Academic Freedom" (1990) reviews the Supreme Court's struggle to define obscenity (a form of speech that is not constitutionally protected) and shows the degree to which the idea eludes definition. Although many declare they know obscenity when they see it, no one has yet crafted a definition sufficiently narrow to capture the thing itself and leave unfettered works that are clearly of socially redeeming value.

According to the Supreme Court's deliberations, a particular work can be found obscene only if it lacks "serious . . . artistic . . . value." Since artistic form and content are inextricably intertwined, it is difficult to apply this criterion. Scurrilous language can be put to very serious purposes. David Nelson's painting of Mayor Washington in women's underwear, displayed briefly in the School of the Art Institute of Chicago before it was destroyed, or Carolee Schneemann's performance art piece *Interior Scroll,* in which she stands naked and draws a scroll from her vagina—to cite two particularly controversial recent works—cannot be dismissed as lewd or without seriousness, no matter how shocking some find the language and images. Both employ parodic means and irony to offer a critique of cultural institutions.

It is difficult to imagine that the obscene can be set apart from the pure with any degree of ease. Censorious spirits as well as many reasonable people are quick to take umbrage at displays of flesh or provocative, sexually explicit language, but the history of art is full of examples that show that such images and words are not intrinsically low or unserious, but are often used to express the highest of ideas and to touch the spirit. Although reasonable people have a right to take exception to such works, perhaps on grounds of good taste or from deeply held religious beliefs, they do not have the right to deny others access to these works.

Federal Funding and the Arts. In the late 1980s a number of issues surfaced nationally that focused attention on the role of the artist in higher education. Among the most prominent was the political quarrel surrounding Congress's amendment to reauthorize the funding of the National Endowment for the Arts and the National Endowment for the Humanities (see Stern, 1990). When these two endowments were first created during the Johnson administration, Americans strongly supported public funding for the arts, believing that the promotion of art and culture was a proper object of national policy and that it was essential to the well-being of our society. This sentiment was due in part to a Kennedy-era pride in American culture, which was seen as having surpassed a European culture that had fallen prey to Fascism. At the time of its creation, the framers of the legislation knew well the need to insulate the process of awarding grants from political pressures. Alas, by the 1980s this objective no longer appeared compelling to many.

During the Republican administrations of the 1980s the country witnessed an increased cry for cutbacks in federal spending, particularly in the area of the arts. Some highly publicized and very provocative works of art became a rallying point for the religious right, who denounced as obscene the artwork of Andres Serrano, Robert Mapplethorpe, and the artists who came to be known as the "NEA Four": Jane Finley, Tim Miller, Holly Hughes, and John Fleck (Phelan, 1991). (For readers who wish to know more about these issues and cases, the July–August 1990 issue of *Academe* offers a useful source of information. It includes an essay by Sheldon Hackney, currently the chairman of the National Endowment for the Humanities. John Frohnmayer's 1993 book *Leaving Town Alive,* written upon his leaving office as the embattled chairman of the National Endowment of the Arts, provides an additional perspective on these events.)

Andres Serrano's work, entitled *Piss Christ,* displayed a plastic crucifix immersed in a bucket of what the artist described to be his own urine. The photographs of Mapplethorpe's that occasioned the greatest outcry involved homoerotic images—one involving sadomasochism, another depicting a black and a white model embracing each other. Jane Finley's now infamous performance art piece was widely rumored to show her eating excrement and rubbing her body with it.

A pattern of retaliation against those museums and universities that housed these controversial works of art became evident, and some of the consequences remain with us today. Just this past year, the level of funding offered to the National Endowment for the Arts and for grants to artists within universities was reduced from recommended levels as a consequence of political battles in Congress. This year, the new Congress will consider eliminating such funding entirely. Consequently, it is not uncommon to hear professors and artists on campus reflect on whether it is wise to bring a controversial performance artist to campus, or whether they should submit grant money for a project that is likely to be judged politically incorrect. These are not healthy times for us.

In many of the most publicized cases, cries to ban artworks came from the religious right, from the Catholic League for Religious and Civil Rights, and from the American Family Association. These groups expressed their desire to suppress offensive art and to compel conformity with their religious convictions. There are ways to be sensitive to these concerns or these groups without acquiescing to their beliefs. Teachers and directors of artistic productions are quite practiced in sensing an audience's mood. When staging a highly controversial play, it might be wise to provide alternative arenas for discussion of the work's ideas and to allow conflicting views to be presented. In advertising such productions, educators can use program notes to contextualize the issues, and they can warn the audience that some may find the work's ideas, images, or language offensive. Administrators can take advantage of the concept of institutional neutrality (see "Academic Freedom and Artistic Expression," 1990) to clarify the institution's relationship to the ideas of its faculty and student members.

Institutional Neutrality. In order to ensure an environment of academic freedom, ideas of all kinds, however loathsome, must be allowed a free forum for debate. Consequently, an institution must not fetter or intrude upon that debate; too often, an administration statement repudiating certain ideas carries far too much weight, chilling discussion. This is not to say that administrators do not often find themselves on the firing line, facing a public demand that the institution defend itself because of the practices or ideas of one of its members. However, a review of many cases shows that a university administration is best served if it reminds the public of its central mission—to foster a climate conducive to intellectual inquiry and the discovery of new knowledge. Such a climate exists when ideas are allowed to be aired and rebutted. Ideas that are suppressed or silenced too often fester, emerging in more fearful manifestations.

In its 1990 statement "Academic Freedom and Artistic Expression," the AAUP and its Wolf Trap Conference co-sponsors wrote about accountability and the concept of institutional neutrality:

> Artistic performances and exhibitions in academic institutions encourage artistic creativity, expression, learning, and appreciation. The institutions do not thereby endorse the specific artistic presentations, nor do the presentations necessarily represent the institution. This principle of institutional neutrality does not relieve institutions of general responsibility for maintaining professional and educational standards, but it does mean that institutions are not responsible for the attitudes expressed in specific artistic works any more than they would be for the content of other instruction, scholarly publication, or invited speeches. Correspondingly, those who present artistic work should not represent themselves or their work as speaking for the institution and should otherwise fulfill their educational and professional responsibilities (pp. 35–36).

The Wolf Trap Statement on Academic Freedom and Artistic Expression

In 1990, when the Mapplethorpe row was at its peak and the controversy over the Mayor Washington portrait was still in full swing, the American Association of University Professors (AAUP) endorsed a statement on academic freedom and artistic expression that had been formulated at a conference it sponsored in conjunction with Wolf Trap and other arts organizations ("Academic Freedom and Artistic Expression," 1990). The statement asserted that, insofar as a teacher instructs about art in the classroom—generally verbally but increasingly with the aid of visual and acoustic media to illustrate ideas—the teacher is guaranteed the right to "free search for truth and its exposition" in order to promote the common good.

The Wolf Trap statement went on to balance the rights of the artist and teacher to make and display artwork with the rights of others in the campus community who argue that they are involuntarily subjected to artwork they find offensive and which violates their rights to privacy. The report further stated that "when academic institutions offer exhibitions or performances to the public, they should ensure that the rights of the presenters and the audience are not impaired by a 'heckler's veto' from those who may be offended by the presentation. Academic institutions should ensure that those who choose to view or attend may do so without interference. Mere presentation in a public place does not create a 'captive audience.' Institutions may reasonably designate specific places as generally available or unavailable for exhibits or performances" ("Academic Freedom and Artistic Expression," 1990, p. 36).

In taking this position, the framers of the statement were not in complete sympathy with a recent judicial ruling: in *Piarowski* v. *Illinois Community College* (1985), the court permitted eight controversial stained-glass windows contributed by Piarowski, chairman of the art department at Illinois Community College, to be removed from the main floor of one of the principal buildings on campus to a fourth-floor room near where the art classes were located. In this case and others like it, the courts have given more weight to the rights of the public—who claim that their viewing a work is involuntary—than to the right of the individual artist to have his or her work seen. In the case cited above, the court was able to reason in this manner because the argument turned on an art-for-art's-sake description of the work. Had Piarowski argued that his depiction of brown women in various servile and sexually graphic postures was a political statement, it would have been harder for the court to strike a tenable compromise that preserved the artist's First Amendment right to have the work viewed on campus while permitting the institution to calm the public outcry by moving the work to a far less central and visible place.

Regulation of time, place, and manner of display or speech has a long and justified tradition under the law. The AAUP's "Academic Freedom and Artistic Expression" statement (1990) expanded on the idea of "reasonable content-neutral regulation of the 'time, place, and manner' of presentations," stating that such regulation should be developed and maintained. But the statement went on to caution academic institutions to ensure that "regulations and procedures do not impair freedom of expression or discourage creativity by subjecting artistic works to tests of propriety or ideology" (p. 35). Recent experiences on campus are testing the feasibility of honoring this injunction.

Institutions of higher education need to be especially careful to ensure that such regulation is indeed completely content-neutral. In many recent cases the regulation of the location of an exhibit has justifiably been a source of concern to artists on campuses. Too often it is only provocative—often homoerotic or politically disquieting—subject matter that occasions such regulation. In one case an exhibit in the lobby of a theater, intended as a prelude to the antiwar play the theater was staging, was ordered dismantled because it was said to be offensive to people standing outside the theater, who could see its violent images through the glass. Faculty members would not have so easily acquiesced to a demand to alter a written prelude to an anti-war text. This play was being produced in a designated theater on campus. It hardly seems legitimate to permit the rights of persons standing outside the theater to outweigh the rights of those who are integrally involved in the institutional mission of the college—the play was staged for instructional purposes and exhibited in a space that is more rightly viewed as an extension of the classroom than as a public space. In this case, as in several others previously cited, it was the ideological content of the artwork that sparked the furor. In such cases it is especially important that the educational community unite behind the principle of academic freedom and not move too quickly to defuse a situation at the expense of artistic expression.

A publication by Robert K. Poch (1993) criticizes the Wolf Trap statement, saying that it largely ignores the difficulties that sometimes arise concerning artistic expression. Citing legally permissible limitations on artistic freedom and the display of works of art and reminding the reader that institutions of higher education would run afoul of the law were they to allow images of child pornography to be shown, Poch sets forth a list of "considerations and recommendations" that may prove useful to institutions in formulating policy. Included in his list are a number of suggestions alluded to earlier in this chapter: that artistic expression found by the courts to be obscene is not constitutionally protected; that institutions of higher education can post statements at the entrance to galleries or theaters or in program notes, stating that the artwork is not necessarily endorsed by the institution and does not necessarily represent its views; that institutions can designate alternate sites for the display of sexually explicit, but not obscene, material. A final suggestion is that institutions hold campuswide seminars, debates, or discussions to coincide with the display or performance of "highly provocative artistic expression" (p. 51).

Many of these suggestions are already widely practiced. Walter P. Metzger, a historian of academic freedom, has long argued that institutions should take advantage of "institutional neutrality," a concept which holds that an institution is not responsible for the ideas of its members. However, institutions must be judicious in their application of this neutrality. A warning about sexually explicit material may be a wise practice for administrators and directors of university theaters; however, when the idea is extended to teachers and to the content of art courses, it becomes dangerous. Many arts educators would also decry the overuse of prior warnings about the kind of material that is to be seen in university theaters.

Limitations on the Place and Manner of Performances, Exhibitions, and Displays

How can teachers and institutions provide an environment in which artistic ideas can flourish, while at the same time addressing the demand that the academic environment be free of sexual and racial harassment or that it conform to standards of good taste or to religious values? Should artworks found to be deeply offensive, though not pornographic or obscene, be removed or at the very least subjected to limitations on their exhibition? Does the students' "right to know" about the content of a course or an exhibit trump professors' rights to determine how and in what manner they will offer instruction or exhibit a work of art? In other words, is the experience of an artistic work so totally compromised by a prior warning about its content that professors should resist these kinds of measures?

The question of whether or not an institution behaves in a responsible manner and in conformity with academic freedom when it relocates or removes a work of art—or otherwise restricts free expression—in response to public pressure is complex. For example, some feminists question whether women should have to look at images of themselves as rendered by "the male gaze." The female nude, they argue, exploits women by objectifying them and appropriating the forms of representation that construct them. Must oppressed groups reaffirm the works of their oppressors, or can they not demand that such works be excluded from consideration? Various minority groups advance similar arguments. For those raised in a tradition of academic freedom, this question is easily answered with a resounding "No." One group may not suppress the ideas or expression of another group—not if they wish to preserve a climate of academic freedom. Rather, each point of view—feminist or multicultural or whatever—must battle openly, no matter how uncomfortably, with other points of view, no matter how odious. Educators and artists can certainly express their ideas, but their insistence on the rightness of their own views cannot justify their silencing others.

Two other cases may serve as illustrative. One occurred at the University of Michigan Law School in November of 1993. The other took place at Northwestern University. The closing of an art exhibit that was part of an academic conference on prostitution forced a debate on campus about free speech, pornography, feminism, and censorship. In this case two of the artists, former prostitutes, chose to show a videotape that showed them practicing their trade. Antipornography speakers indicated that they would not participate in the conference if speakers presenting a different view were present. In addition, there were students, faculty members, and feminists who opposed the exhibit, wishing to see pornography banned. Their efforts were fueled by the scholarly work of Catharine MacKinnon, a professor of law at the university and a pioneer of the movement to ban pornography because it allegedly incites sexual violence against women. Several law students learned about the controversial videotape—called ethnographic by its producers and pornographic by its opponents—and removed it from the exhibit. The exhibit was ultimately closed down; the curator of the gallery decried the selective censorship of one part of the exhibit. Later, the law school agreed to display the portion of the exhibit that was removed as part of a symposium on feminist theory and issues of sexual expression and censorship.

This case reenacted a pattern of events that are increasingly common on campuses. The boundaries between high and low art are becoming blurred. In the case at the University of Michigan, the idea of sex work as artwork was one of the issues that sparked the furor. Annie Sprinkle, once a 42nd Street porno star, now a performance artist, is another figure whose presence as an artist challenges ideas about high and low art. Much of the best of today's art is "found" art, art made from ordinary commodities or developed in the streets; these works possess a sense of urgency, often addressing gender and diversity issues on other campuses. Faculty and students alike are experiencing the devastation surrounding AIDS, particularly in the artistic and theater communities. Art about AIDS is created on many campuses, and much of it is both political as well as therapeutic and aesthetic. With the exhibition of ethnographic practices and the presentation of collections of the narratives and art of minorities on campuses, it is likely that more, not fewer, events like those at the University of Michigan, San Francisco State University, and Vanderbilt will occur in the next few years.

The second case, at Northwestern University, is an example of a more modest controversy. This event did not lead to either the canceling of a production or an upsurge of homophobic sentiment on a campus. It is included here because it points to the kind of question that vexes theater directors, student actors, audiences, and teachers with considerable frequency. In this case, Frank Galati—director of the Broadway version of *The Grapes of Wrath* and an actor, director, screenwriter, and teacher—chose to develop a composite script of writings of Marguerite Duras to be incorporated into Northwestern University's Theater and Interpretation Center's 1992–1993 season. His script centered on a story by Duras, "Blue Eyes, Black Hair," weaving in materials from other stories and from Duras's diaries. The central story deals with homoeroticism as well as heterosexual love, and the language, although highly lyrical, is also graphic in its description of certain sex acts generally considered "perverse." The staged production contained no nudity, and there was almost no touching between the actors and actresses; rather, the audience was caressed by language and witnessed stage actions illuminated by stark, yet simple lighting which made them think, or imagine, that things were being shown to them that were, in fact, not actually enacted. The director allowed the production to be used in a class on the Integrated Arts. Students, many of them freshman, were required to attend the performance and write about it. At the time this requirement was made, Galati had not completed his selection of all the stories to be included, nor had he fully charted the directorial devices and choreography he would use. Sometime toward the middle of the quarter in which the show was to be staged, the script was finalized and the actors began to work with Galati. Word leaked that the show involved sexually explicit language and that its subject matter was controversial. The teachers in the Integrated Arts class had required students to read the script as well as to see the show. Some faculty believed the class should be warned about the material and told that they did not have to see it should they find it objectionable. Other faculty argued that it would be misleading to characterize the material in this way in advance of the performance, and that to do so would be detrimental to the educational process. The teachers chose to say nothing and let the process evolve.

When the show opened, many audience members walked out, some protesting that "absolutely nothing happened in the show," and others indignantly describing the work as "pure filth." Still others described the production to be one of the finest works they had ever seen at Northwestern University and one of Galati's greatest artistic achievements. The university stood behind the production, and Galati wrote an open letter to the audience, to be distributed and discussed by students *after* the show had been seen. Later a part of this letter was reproduced in a university magazine, *Dialogue* (1993), an appropriate forum in which to answer alumnae and others who had raised questions about the production.

This scenario illustrates some of the problems that teachers of fine and performing arts constantly face. They must try to strike a balance between the need to encourage creativity and explore ideas, no matter how provocative, and the need to try to respect the rights of others. Academic freedom protections provide them with a concept that makes it possible for them to pursue their work, particularly in an era in which art is political in nature and conflicting ideas abound.

Should the Protections of Academic Freedom Extend to the Arts?

Before concluding this essay, which has largely confined its attention to recent attempts to curtail artistic expression on campuses and the part that academic freedom can play in addressing and resolving these issues, we need to consider the fundamental question of whether academic freedom legitimately applies to the artist in the university. Edward Shils, for example, has argued that academic freedom protects the quest for truth. Since art, as understood by rationalists, does not find truth, the protections of academic freedom would not extend to artists.

A variation on this argument surfaced during discussions between members of the AAUP's Committee A on Academic Freedom and Tenure. The discussion involved an argument about whether artistic speech merits the special kind of protection some would accord to political speech. Ought scholars of academic freedom be particularly sensitive to the special needs of artistic expression? Some feel that First Amendment protections should be particularly firm in regard to works with political subject matter, while many would afford less protection to erotic speech. Speech that addresses the emotions and takes as its subject bodily functions, carnal desire, and the erotic is often considered by the law, as well as by philosophy and religion, to be less worthy and less in need of protection. In fact, many argue that such speech borders on the obscene. Such thinking would not argue for a special kind of privilege for artistic speech.

Even the capacity of art to delight and instruct, which constructs its social value and clearly locates it in the interest of the common good, sometimes lends to its devaluation. To the extent that its instructional component is generally accepted—or to put it another way, to the extent the art is "safe"—its capacity to move people is taken for granted and untroubling. But when the artist innovates and goes against the common grain, then art's particular capacity to excite emotion is used as a reason to isolate the artist and accord art lesser protection than intellectual expression.

On the other hand, in times of extreme political repression, when political movements are forced underground, cultural and artistic revivals sometimes occur. For example, upon the defeat of the Home Rule Bill in Ireland in the waning years of the nineteenth century, the political movement went underground while the Gaelic Revival and the Irish theater flourished. A similar argument points to the value of art in shaping cultural values, maintaining that artistic speech is often deemed "dangerous" precisely because it masks political speech. Both arguments affirm the political and cultural significance of artistic expression.

Many scholars argue that it is a mistake to treat the erotic as essentially nonpolitical and less serious than other kinds of speech. Rather, many theorists argue that hard-core pornography fulfills a very complex social function and may have profound political implications. Art may reveal "truths of the human spirit," whether glorious or base, that scientific and political discourse inadequately express. In short, perhaps it is limiting to believe that only scientific or political deliberations deserve the full protections of academic freedom. Would it not be more appropriate to follow the guidance of the original founders of the AAUP in 1915, who defined academic freedom from the perspective of the profession? Such an approach would place artistic expression on the same footing as intellectual inquiry and would provide both activities equal protections under standards of academic freedom within the university.

Few would argue that the college or university *teacher* of the arts—whether visual, theatrical, musical, or dance—is not afforded the protections of academic freedom. The AAUP's "1940 Statement of Principles on Academic Freedom and Tenure" (1990) provides them with full freedom "in research and in the publication of the results," as well as "in the classroom in discussing their subject." The cautionary words included in this statement, entreating teachers to enjoy the privileges of academic freedom but to exercise care "not to introduce into their teaching controversial matter which has no relation to their subject," applies equally to teachers in the arts as it does to teachers in other disciplines. What has been especially vexatious in recent discussions about teachers' and artists' rights to academic freedom has flowed from the important differences that separate the teacher and scholar of art from the actual artist. The AAUP's statement on academic freedom clearly protects the teacher of art just as much as the teacher of science. But what is difficult to judge is the extent to which academic freedom protects the making of art, as distinct from teaching about it.

This leads us to the question of the extent to which a visual artist's creative work is analogous to a scholar's publication. This question has become commonplace among scholars of academic freedom in addressing how academic freedom has a bearing on the creation and production of art on campus. It is a dubious question—it sheds little light on the issue it purports to address, while revealing rather tellingly the prejudice many scholars hold against the artist. The question is ill-posed, because the creation of art is best compared to research, not publication (likewise, campus art exhibits are best compared to campus public lectures rather than to publications). As to the prejudice that underlies this confusion, the artist's role in higher education is relatively marginal if measured by the status of art faculty in colleges and universities. While the culture lauds their performance, very often artists appointed to faculty positions hold nontenured or adjunct appointments rather than full-fledged tenure-track positions. Some institutions of higher education are distinguished by the strengths of their commitment to arts education and arts faculty. But the large majority of research universities, public and private, as well as many liberal arts colleges, benefit greatly from their arts programs and from the presence of widely acclaimed artists on campus, while treating their arts faculty as lesser professionals than other faculty members.

In the case of scholarly research and publication, the scholar is assured protection insofar as he or she performs research and inquires about ideas, no matter how offensive those ideas are. The dissemination of research in the form of articles or books is also protected against overt censorship. Academicians are all too familiar with the history of attempts to ban the publication of books, and they are accustomed to argue forcibly for the freedom to publish. However, they would note that there is no inherent right to publish; that is, though one may write what one wishes, publishers need not publish works they consider unworthy or unsuitable.

Accordingly, one may reasonably argue that art faculty have no inherent right to free expression *in a particular venue*. Furthermore, the teacher of an art or theater class who wishes to exhibit or produce student work so that it can be seen not only by the academic community but also by the public cannot expect these works to be free of all restraints. In short, the rights of the "publisher" and the prospective viewer of the work must also be considered. Consequently, the question of whether student or faculty artwork should be placed "in-the-face" of anyone on campus who happens to chance upon it raises vexing issues that cannot be resolved simply by an appeal to the AAUP's statement on academic freedom.

Nonetheless, in distinguishing acceptable from unacceptable grounds for limiting creative expression, the same sorts of criteria apply as for scholarly publications and presentations. Generally accessible faculty and student artwork and theatrical productions on campus, like the generally accessible seminars and such to which they are best compared, may be subjected to rules. Such rules may include qualitative standards, provisions for participation to be "refereed" or "juried," and general regulations on "time, place, and manner." However, such rules should not be selectively applied according to arbitrary determinations of whether a specific communication is scientific, political, or artistic. Above all, rules should not impose, and should protect against, "tests of propriety or ideology" ("Academic Freedom and Artistic Expression," p. 35.) It is precisely these sorts of tests that underlie most controversies regarding artistic expression on the campus. It is precisely these sorts of tests that must be resisted if the arts, and the academy, are to flourish.

References

"Academic Freedom and Artistic Expression." In *AAUP Policy Documents and Reports*. Washington, D.C.: American Association of University Professors, 1990, pp. 35–36.

Bostick, A. "Sex Photos Lead to Hot Debate." *Tennessean*, Feb. 24, 1993, pp. 1A–2A.

"A Conflict About Art." *The Nashville Banner*, Feb. 19, 1993, p. A-8.

Frohnmayer, J. *Leaving Town Alive: Confessions of an Artist Warrior*. Boston: Houghton Mifflin, 1993.

Hackney, S. "The NEA Under Attack: Resisting the Big Chill." *Academe*, 1990, 76 (4), 17.

"1940 Statement of Principles on Academic Freedom and Tenure." In *AAUP Policy Documents and Reports*. Washington, D.C.: American Association of University Professors, 1990, pp. 3–10.

O'Neil, R. M. "Artistic Freedom and Academic Freedom." *Law and Contemporary Problems*, 1990, 53 (3), 177–193.

Parsons, C. "Fury of the 1st." *Nashville Scene*, Mar. 4, 1993, pp. 5–6.

Phelan, P. "Money Talks, Again." *TDR*, 1991, 35 (3), 131–141.

Piarowski v. Illinois Community College [759 F. 2d 625 (1985)].

Poch, R. K. *Academic Freedom in American Higher Education: Rights, Responsibilities and Limitations* (ASHE-ERIC Higher Education Report No. 4). Washington, D.C.: George Washington University, 1993.

"San Francisco State Destroys Malcolm X Mural After Furor." *New York Times*, May 27, 1994, p. A10.

Stern, C. S. "Artistic Freedom and Federal Funding." *Academe*, 1990, 76 (4), 56.

CAROL SIMPSON STERN *is professor of performance studies and dean of the graduate school at Northwestern University. She is director of the integrated arts program at Northwestern University and is past president of the American Association of University Professors.*

Denial of the academic freedom necessary for participation in academic governance generally reflects lack of institutional recognition of faculty professionalism.

"Dirty Little Cases": Academic Freedom, Governance, and Professionalism

Sheila Slaughter

This chapter examines "dirty little cases,"[1] academic freedom cases from 1970–1990 that were filed with the American Association of University Professors (AAUP) because the colleges and universities involved did not recognize widely accepted professional norms. In these dirty little cases, institutional managers dismissed faculty members as a consequence of their participation in academic governance.

Governance—providing faculty participation in institutional decision making—merits the protection of academic freedom because faculty possess the expertise necessary to make informed decisions about curricula and to evaluate students and peers based on that knowledge. Faculty participation in hiring, tenure, and promotion decisions is especially important given the necessity for detailed knowledge of specific fields in making these decisions. Collectively, faculty members are the repository for professional norms that inform the judgement of communities of scholars, a judgement that makes education possible. Administrators who show no regard for professional values as expressed by faculty in the governance process deny themselves the best available advice and counsel.

From a theoretical point of view, dirty little cases are interesting because they run counter to professionalization theory, which offers the dominant explanation for why institutional managers have granted professors powers of governance. The two major schools of professionalization theory are the "trait" and "process" schools. Both trait and process theories of professionalization see professors, by virtue of their expertise, as knowing more about how to discover and deliver knowledge than administrators, who lack the requisite specialization.

The trait school sees professors and other professionals as acquiring certain characteristics through education or practice that entitles them to professional status. Among those traits frequently mentioned are command of a body of knowledge informed by theory, altruistic or non-self-interested interactions with clients or patients, a code of ethics, and autonomy (Greenwood, 1957; Etzioni, 1969; Moore, 1970). According to the trait school, autonomy is a characteristic of a professional. Faculty who have acquired the necessary traits are automatically granted governance rights that enable them to make relatively autonomous decisions, even though they are employees of colleges and universities as well as professionals.

Process theories of professionalization are less concerned with traits and characteristics and pay more attention to power and social-class relations that shape professions. Process theories of professionalization do not see particular traits as conferring autonomy; instead, these theories see organized professionals with strong market potential negotiating with resource holders, political parties, legislators, and proponents of social movements to win concessions that grant professors autonomy (Larson, 1977; Friedson, 1986). Process theorists differ from trait theorists in that they see the collective organizational skills that professionals use in the political process as being as important to achieving professional status as specific traits or clusters of traits, including command of a body of knowledge informed by theory.

Neither the trait nor the process school of professionalization deals with the question of why some faculty, three-quarters of a century after professors as a group gained a good deal of autonomy with respect to their institutions, are today denied autonomy and privileges of self-governance. After presenting data that dramatically illustrate the degree to which some professors are *not* granted autonomy and governance privileges, I will reconsider the explanations provided by professionalization theory.

From my analysis of dirty little cases, five main points emerge. First, the data suggest that not all colleges and universities are equally likely to honor claims to professional autonomy and self-governance and that we can predict with some certainty which institutions are most likely to disregard professional norms. Second, administrators involved in these cases treat professors as employees, not professionals. These administrators' treatment of professors is more like that of nineteenth-century factory bosses with unchecked power over their wage-earning workers than that of modern managers of complex organizations dealing with highly educated staff members. Such administrators violate widely prevailing institutional norms. In most colleges and universities, administrators recognize professors' right to speak, even if they do not recognize a concomitant administrative responsibility to listen. But at institutions where dirty little cases have occurred, professors who spoke out were treated as insubordinate. Third, in these cases faculty find it extremely difficult to establish any boundaries for administrators through collective action because of the imbalance of power between the two groups. Fourth, prolonged conflict between faculty members and administrations, often lasting many years and sometimes for more than a decade, have frequently led to severe factionalization within the professional work force, creating an almost unendurable climate on campus that is counterproductive to education and scholarship. Fifth, although approximately half of these cases have been resolved, the institutional peace established was often fragile and depended on the re-education of faculty and administrators, as well as on establishing a collective process to rebuild a modicum of good will and trust.

Data and Methods

As I read through the AAUP cases from 1970 to 1990, I categorized as dirty little cases all those in which professors were fired because they criticized the administration publicly; because they tried to organize a faculty senate, an AAUP chapter, or a union; or because they brought a grievance. Dirty little cases were cases in which faculty were denied an institutional voice and an authentic stake in governance. Twenty-nine cases fell into this category. I placed these cases into the broad context of the total numbers and types of academic freedom cases reported in *Academe* from 1970 to 1990 (for a full discussion of data and method, see Slaughter 1980, 1987, 1993, in press). I analyzed the type of institution at which these cases occurred as well as their geographical location. I identified the patterns that characterized them, and present six representative cases, highlighting their common features.

Context of the Cases

Although dirty little cases did not account for the largest numbers of dismissed faculty, they were the most prevalent of all the types of cases in the sample and accounted for the third largest numbers of dismissals during the twenty-year period studied. From 1970 to 1990, Committee A reported 1,589 faculty dismissals (Slaughter 1987, in press). Financial exigency or retrenchment and restructuring cases accounted for the largest numbers of dismissals (84 percent). A single case was responsible for the largest number of dismissals for financial exigency, the mass dismissals of faculty members (1,000 dismissals, or 63 percent of the faculty) at City University of New York (CUNY) due to a municipal fiscal crisis. The second largest number of firings in the twenty-year period stemmed from civil liberties-type cases (political action, religious action, freedom of speech).[2] These cases resulted in 104 dismissals (6 percent if the CUNY financial exigency case is included, 18 percent if it is not). Most of these cases stemmed from the political ferment of the late 1960s and early 1970s and were clustered in the early part of the 1970s. If the CUNY dismissals are discounted, then the twenty-nine dirty little cases accounted for 12 percent of all dismissals over the twenty-year period. If the CUNY dismissals are included, dirty little cases constituted approximately 3 percent of the dismissals.

In the 1980s, dirty little cases resulted in the largest absolute number of dismissals after financial exigency or restructuring cases. Overall, dirty little cases were most regular, even more so than financial exigency or restructuring cases, which were concentrated in the late 1970s and middle 1980s. Dirty little cases occurred every year but four in the twenty years under consideration. The greatest number of persons fired in a single year was sixteen; there were only four years in which more than five persons were fired. The total number of faculty fired in dirty little cases was sixty-three. These cases were a routine part of academic life at some institutions.

Dirty little cases were generally concentrated in undistinguished institutions at the lower end of the postsecondary prestige hierarchy. Using the Carnegie Commission on Higher Education (1973, 1987) classification schemes, the largest number (eight, or 28 percent) were at two-year and community colleges. Next were medical or specialized (business) colleges (seven, or 24 percent); two of these were colleges of osteopathic medicine, and one was a college of optometry. Although medical schools might seem anomalous, given that they are prestigious, they—like schools of osteopathy and optometry—often follow an institute rather than a collegial model of governance. The institute model concentrates power in a single administrator who is sometimes quite dictatorial. Six dirty little cases were at liberal arts II (21 percent), six (21 percent) were at comprehensives. Of the six 4-year liberal arts colleges, five were religious. Of the twelve liberal arts and comprehensive cases, five were at historically black institutions. Two of the dirty little cases (7 percent) were at doctoral granting institutions. Of the twenty-nine dirty little cases, fourteen were at private schools and fourteen were at public schools. One institution was a hybrid, classified as both private and public. Only two of the twenty-nine schools were unionized. One institution had very recently established an American Federation of Teachers chapter; the other had a house union, affiliated with no state or national body.

With regard to geographical location, thirteen (45 percent) were in the South, eight (28 percent) in the Mid-Atlantic states, five (17 percent) in the Midwest, two (7 percent) in the West, and one (3 percent) in the New England states. Until the 1970s, the South was arguably the most culturally, economically, and educationally isolated region of the U.S. The large number of cases in the South in the 1970s might be due to the integration of the South's institutions of higher education into the national postsecondary system, and the consequent intrainstitutional conflicts. During the 1970s and 1980s, a relatively large number of Ph.D.'s were produced, but relatively few faculty positions opened. As a result, Southern institutions may have hired larger numbers of Ph.D.'s from outside, and these new faculty members may have precipitated demands for a greater voice in governance.

The cases displayed a number of common features. By definition, dirty little cases were those in which faculty members tried to secure an institutional voice. In the majority of cases (fifteen) faculty were dismissed merely for being openly critical of the administration. In three cases faculty members went further than criticism and attempted to organize a faculty senate. In another three cases faculty members were fired because of their membership in the AAUP. In two cases faculty members attempted to organize collective bargaining; in another two they were dismissed for bringing grievances. In many cases (nine, or 31 percent), the institutions had no tenure system. To put this figure in perspective, the degree to which tenure is an academic norm must be understood: 25.5 percent of community colleges have tenure; 97 percent of four-year institutions have tenure (Smith, 1984). At community colleges, the absence of tenure was not exceptional; at four-year institutions it was very unusual. In almost all cases, the institutions had inadequate, if any, due process or procedures to guide giving notice of termination.

Specific Dirty Little Cases

Given the similarity of these cases, I selected cases to present here based on the type of institution represented rather than the type of case. I present a case from a community college; a medical-specialized institution; a four-year, historically black institution; a four-year private college; a four-year religious college; and a four-year comprehensive public college. Although these cases do not differ dramatically, they provide texture and detail to illuminate the problems faced by faculty members at institutions that fail to give professors any institutional voice or a modicum of professional autonomy.

Laredo Community College. Lyndon Daly was a tenured professor of history who led his colleagues in creating a faculty senate and establishing an AAUP chapter. He fell into debt and was hospitalized for severe heart trouble. He was terminated before he could inform the college of his illness. The president maintained that Daly was dismissed because he did not meet his classes. Daly insisted that he was fired because he organized the faculty so they could participate in institutional governance. Shortly after Daly's dismissal, Mr. Kemp Dixon, president of the AAUP chapter, and five other nontenured members of the faculty, all AAUP members, were asked to resign or were not reappointed. Students at Laredo protested the dismissals, to no avail. The Laredo board of trustees said the six AAUP members were dismissed because their activities did not "fit . . . in with the philosophy of Laredo Junior College" (Committee A, 1970). The members of the board of trustees thought the professors were competent, had engaged in no improprieties, and were highly regarded by students.

The Laredo case illustrates the power of the president to define institutional reality in some situations. Despite the obvious relationship between Daly's activism and his dismissal, the president was able to deny any causal connection between Daly's effort to establish institutional governance and his firing, asserting instead that the dismissal was based on grounds—missing classes—that harmed the ability of the institution to deliver its product: education. The board, in firing other active faculty members, demonstrated its complete control over the institution, revealing that it regarded faculty members as mere employees, not professors possessed of special knowledge crucial to the activity of education; nor did it regard them as professionals who shared norms, values, and traditions that had a bearing on institutional affairs. The dismissed professors were regarded as competent, but mastery of a field and ability to teach effectively was not sufficient to compensate for their transgressions against managerial authority. The AAUP eventually removed Laredo Community College from its censure list. Professor Daly died, making the compensation issue moot, and a new administration, which wanted censure removed, established tenure and developed safeguards and procedures that complied with AAUP guidelines.

Illinois College of Optometry. Professors Alexander and Shansky, who held Ph.D.'s in psychology from the University of Washington and Syracuse University, respectively, had served the college over seven years but were still on term contracts, as were all faculty members. They attempted to establish a faculty senate and adopt AAUP guidelines as institutional personnel policy.

Alexander was chair of the faculty organizing committee. Alexander and Shansky regularly confronted the administrator who simultaneously held the position of dean and chair of the division in which they worked. They dealt with him in his capacity as dean on issues of governance, and in his capacity as division chair on issues of curriculum. Given that the administrator did not have a degree in an area related to the division specialization, he was somewhat uncertain of his authority. At a meeting with the dean/chair dealing with curriculum, Alexander and Shansky walked out in protest over the time frame in which the issue would be handled. The dean/chair and the president warned the faculty members that their behavior was unacceptable, and immediately rescheduled the meeting for the afternoon of the same day of the walkout. Alexander and Shansky claimed prior commitments, did not attend, and were fired.

The charges brought against Alexander and Shansky were "irresponsibility, insubordination, and evidence of an unwillingness to cooperate in furthering the purposes of the College" (Committee A, 1982, p. 20a). They were summarily dismissed: "The professors were escorted from the College by uniformed campus security police and were subsequently allowed to retrieve their effects only in the presence of the police and the College legal counsel" (Committee A, 1982, p. 20a). The professors filed charges with the National Labor Relations Board (NLRB), to no avail. They instituted a civil suit, but failed to win a preliminary injunction to forestall dismissal. The Illinois College of Optometry remains on the AAUP censure list.

As in the Laredo case, the Illinois College of Optometry case pointed to the unfettered power of administrators at some institutions to define events. When Alexander and Shansky, who possess Ph.D.'s from elite institutions rather than the osteopathic degrees held by the school's administrators, took issue with an insecure dean/chair over a trivial scheduling issue, the administration was able to accuse them of "insubordination" and have the police physically remove them from the premises, a show of force that undoubtedly dampened the organizing ardor of other faculty. The administrators at the college were operating on an institutional model typical of medical schools, where the director/authority figure holds great power. They were probably unfamiliar with the professional norms informing collegial governance and saw their treatment of Alexander and Shansky as justified.

Talladega College. A number of dirty little cases were at historically African-American institutions. Like faculty at other institutions, faculty at these colleges were attempting to professionalize, and in the process confronted autocratic administrators. In the years after 1965, the demand for African-American faculty at predominantly white institutions grew, creating many more options than were previously available to them. Faculty members with greater market potential probably felt more able to challenge administrators.

Talladega College illustrates the problems encountered by faculty at traditionally African-American institutions. Howard Rogers chaired the social sciences division, which sent a memo to the board of trustees voicing the division's "concern with . . . the general academic environment at the college and a perceived absence of administrative commitment to open dialogue and communication with the faculty, an absence of administrative concern for the integrity of the academic program, . . . and an absence of any administrative vision for the future of this college beyond mere survival" (Committee A, 1986b, p. 7a). The faculty doubted "the capacity of this administration to address these concerns" (Committee A, 1986b, p.7a).

The president charged the faculty with attempting to "preempt [his] office" and "circumvent established lines of communication" (Committee A, 1986b, p.7a). Faculty complaints about the administration were taken up by the Faculty Concerns Committee, which eventually accused the administration of trying to pack the committee with college personnel who did not have voting status in order to secure outcomes sought by the administration. The Faculty Concerns Committee brought these and other charges to the board of trustees, which heard out the faculty members and then gave their full support to the president, delegating to him virtually complete authority for managing the institution. Shortly thereafter, the president terminated the services of Rogers and several other professors who had engaged in criticism of his administration. Two of these professors were locked out of their offices and escorted from the campus by security police. The faculty appealed unsuccessfully to the trustees, and then turned to the courts. The county court judge dismissed their suits, and the case went to appeal. Talladega College remains on the AAUP censure list.

Again, as in the Laredo Junior College and the Illinois College of Optometry cases, the president saw even a request to establish dialogue as an attempt to "preempt" his office, a threat to administrative control and to bureaucratic hierarchy. Again like Laredo, the matter ended up before the board of trustees, and again the board sided with the president, reinforcing rather than diminishing his powers. In these cases the boards, which hold legal authority over the institutions, generally sided with the administrations, further contributing to the adversarial relationship between faculty members and their institutions.

Hillsdale College. Professor Warren Treadgold has a Ph.D. from Harvard in Byzantine Greek history and is the author of many books and monographs. He received his degree at a time when he was "faced with a scarcity of regular faculty positions in the field of his academic specialization" (Committee A, 1988, p.29), so he took a position at Hillsdale College. Hillsdale presents itself to the public as a conservative institution, supporting free-enterprise economic systems and traditional moral values. Hillsdale refuses to accept federal money or to submit information under Title IX, and it has raised a $30 million endowment on the strength of its position with regard to government subvention.

Treadgold was on leave nearly half the time he was at Hillsdale, spending the academic year at institutions such as Berkeley and UCLA. When he was at Hillsdale, he had a reduced teaching load. He was associated with a faction of the Hillsdale faculty that thought the college should use its endowment to raise academic standards and create a Harvard or Amherst of the Midwest. While Treadgold was away, the faction with which he was associated charged the president with personal misconduct. Many faculty thought the charges were unwarranted and disruptive. As a counter to these charges, an administrator began suing a faculty member associated with Treadgold's group for slander. Treadgold, with others of his faction, wrote a letter to the student newspaper, arguing that the administrator's lawsuit was outrageous and should not go to court.

When Treadgold came up for promotion and tenure, he was told by the administration that he did not fit in at Hillsdale. No reasons for the dismissal were given. However, the AAUP investigating committee thought that many faculty and staff members at Hillsdale were disturbed by Treadgold's lack of commitment to the institution, and they surmised that he might have been fired because of a "difference in values and expectations between the typical small liberal arts college and the large research institution" (Committee A, 1988, p. 32). Hillsdale College remains on the AAUP censure list.

The Hillsdale case suggests that institutions where dirty little cases occur are essentially local in orientation, not cosmopolitan. Alvin Gouldner (1957) contrasts local to cosmopolitan faculty members, arguing that some professors are invested in local issues primarily related to institutional well-being while others' more cosmopolitan identities are shaped by the quest for publication and recognition, honors, and awards conferred by external associations, such as organizations of learned disciplines. At research institutions, cosmopolitans are usually more valued than locals. At Hillsdale the reverse was the case, and Treadgold was honored only grudgingly. Many of the institutions at which dirty little cases occur are more local than cosmopolitan, although frequently they do not accord even locals a strong voice in institutional affairs.

Alvernia College. Tullio De Santis, who holds an MFA from the San Francisco Art Institute, was an assistant professor of art at Alvernia. After a colleague fell ill he became the only full-time faculty member in the art department. De Santis thought that he would become chair of the department, but that position was claimed by Sister Magnifica, a nun with no college teaching experience. De Santis and Sister Magnifica had a falling out, and he made criticisms of her to the president. The criticism was vigorous but, according to the AAUP investigating committee, within the bounds of academic discourse. De Santis received no response until the beginning of the fall semester, when he was dismissed. He went to his first class despite his dismissal, but was prevented from entering, and a substitute professor took over. When he asked why he was dismissed, he was informed that he was fired because of his criticism of Sister Magnifica. He attempted to bring a grievance, but was told by the administration that he could not do so because he was already dismissed. The college attorney informed De Santis that he had not been reappointed a year ago, when he failed to sign his contract on time. Although De Santis was unaware of his status, he had been serving on an "at-will" basis since the previous year (Committee A, 1990, p. 68).

Despite the administration's refusal to allow De Santis to file a grievance, the faculty council agreed to hear his claim. They unanimously called for retroactive reinstatement of De Santis, and argued that if dismissal was then deemed necessary, it should be done with due process. Generally, the college's faculty were extremely upset by the dismissal, which highlighted the problems of governance at Alvernia, among which were governance committees listed in the faculty handbook that did not exist in practice. Their dismay at the lack of due process prompted approximately half the full-time faculty to found an AAUP chapter. The college vice-president told faculty with administrative responsibilities who joined the chapter that they would lose their jobs due to a conflict of interest. Two students wrote a letter to the student newspaper that supported the faculty, but the president prevented its publication, violating the college code that the student newspaper should be separate from the administration. The students dropped out of college.

At Alvernia, as at other institutions where dirty little cases occurred, faculty members were denied participation in academic decision making. Unlike some of the cases considered thus far, the faculty at Alvernia were not split into warring factions, but developed a cohesive voice. After De Santis's dismissal, faculty worked with the National Education Association to establish a union, going to court to gain the right to bargain collectively with the administration. However, the Yeshiva decision (*National Labor Relations Board* v. *Yeshiva University,* 1980)—in which the Supreme Court ruled that faculty at private colleges and universities do not have a protected right to collective bargaining because they share decision-making powers with their administration—was used to prevent Alvernia faculty from unionizing.

Despite this setback, faculty at Alvernia remained organized. Their AAUP chapter was instrumental in bringing about a change in management, establishing a faculty senate, and improving institutional procedures. Tullio de Santis got his job back. The AAUP removed Alvernia from its censure list.

University of Northern Colorado. Achal Mehra, a citizen of India, was an assistant professor of communications at the University of Northern Colorado. He was very active in opposing a retrenchment proposal at the university, which ultimately resulted in the dismissal of twenty faculty members (Committee A, 1984). He organized a committee on intellectual freedom, sponsored petitions of no confidence in the president, and called for the president's resignation. While he was engaged in these activities, he had to refile with the U.S. Immigration and Naturalization Service (INS) to renew his nonimmigrant visa. The petition was sent to the university's central administrative office, not to Mehra's department head, and the administration denied that Mehra filled his temporary position better than available U.S. applicants for the job. The administration then withdrew the petition to extend his visa, without telling Mehra or his department, which had voted that Mehra's appointment be renewed and had unanimously recommended that he be department head the following year.

Mehra was arrested by INS officers and placed in detention in Denver. Mehra claimed the administration had used the INS to stifle his criticism of retrenchment. After complicated negotiations, the INS and the administration agreed that Mehra could complete the academic year, after which he would be terminated. During that year he married a U.S. citizen; he then claimed that the administration, which had based its case against him on his immigration status, no longer had grounds for termination, since he was now a citizen. The administration then changed its charges, saying they would not rehire Mehra because he did not show sufficient commitment to the institution since he had made clear to various persons that he wanted to return to India. Mehra moved in federal court for an injunction against the university and the INS (Committee A, 1986a).

The AAUP censured the University of Northern Colorado on two counts: (1) faulty processes used during retrenchment and (2) dismissal of Mehra. When Northern Colorado revamped its policies and procedures, the AAUP removed the first count of censure. The second count was more complicated. Mehra lost his first amendment case in court; indeed, the judge rendered a verdict that required Mehra to recompense the president of Northern Colorado. Mehra did not pay these monies over; he took a job at an Eastern college. When a new administration took over at Northern Colorado, it resolved the Mehra case by inviting Mehra to give a lecture on academic freedom, paying him a stipend, thereby signalling that the episode was over. At that point, the AAUP removed Northern Colorado from the censure list.

As restructuring of postsecondary education becomes more prevalent, intrainstitutional conflict is likely to intensify. Thus far, restructuring has occurred primarily at relatively undistinguished two- and four-year colleges, although an increasing number of research universities are engaging in this process (Slaughter, 1993a). In general, administrators tend to usurp faculty power during restructuring, arrogating curricula decisions to themselves by retaining the final power to say which programs are kept and which programs are cut. The Northern Colorado case, in which a faculty member who spoke out vigorously against retrenchment and restructuring was fired, is probably the exception rather than the rule. Administrators do not need to silence critics, because the process of restructuring gives them powers that weaken faculty self-governance. As restructuring becomes more widespread, governance, especially with regard to curricula and workload, is likely to be eroded, and faculty will find it more difficult to protect their academic freedom (see the special issue on retrenchment, *Journal of Higher Education,* [Slaughter, 1993a]).

Discussion

These twenty-nine dirty little cases suggest that all colleges and universities are not equally likely to honor claims to professional autonomy and self-governance. Generally, the greatest number of dirty little cases were found at institutions toward the lower end of the prestige scale.[3] The two-year sector, which is closest to the common school and is characterized by open-access policies and a "second chance" philosophy, is generally regarded as being on the lowest rung of the prestige ladder. If the cases neatly followed ranking schemes, such as the Carnegie classification, there would have been more dirty little cases at four-year schools than at comprehensives. Instead, the number was the same. There were only a few dirty little cases at doctoral-granting institutions.

Although four-year schools are usually seen as more prestigious than two-year schools, there is great variation among four-year schools' levels of prestige. Some—Amherst, Williams, Vassar, Oberlin—are gateways to elite graduate and professional schools, while most are not. None of the four-year schools at which dirty little cases have occurred are feeders of elite graduate and professional schools. Instead, they are toward the lower end of the status scale within the four-year school sector. The same is true of dirty little cases at comprehensive universities. Although these institutions grant M.A. degrees and some grant doctoral degrees as well, they do not usually have strong connections to elite research universities. Like those four-year colleges at which dirty little cases have taken place, the comprehensives are not near the high end of the status scale within their sector.

As noted earlier, the institutions at which dirty little cases occur are locally oriented. Administrators at these institutions, and sometimes significant numbers of their faculty, do not see associations of learned disciplines and professional associations as a primary frame of reference. They are local in another sense as well. Twenty-three of the twenty-nine institutions (79 percent) are situated in small towns, often quite removed from a metropolitan center. Almost half (45 percent) are in the South, until fairly recently the least urbanized and least unionized region in the country.

In dirty little cases, administrators have usually treated faculty members like employees rather than professionals. They have charged faculty members who wanted to participate in institutional decision making with "insubordination," "troublemaking," even "sedition" (Committee A, 1982). As the AAUP investigating committee remarked in one case, the reasons given by administrators for dismissals were "more appropriate to a military organization or an industrial enterprise than to an institution of higher learning" (Committee A,

1982). The more exact analogy might have been between administrators at institutions where dirty little cases have taken place and heads of firms in a company town. Such administrators are paternalistic and see themselves as entitled to power and competent to deal with all institutional issues. They define themselves as bosses and treat their faculty members as workers. They treat the educational enterprise as an uncomplicated delivery of knowledge, a task so concrete and clearly defined that there is no need for professional expertise.

Assessing faculty members' collective response to bosslike administrators is difficult, because the AAUP case documents do not uniformly report the reaction of faculties as a whole to the various cases. In those cases where the case documents give some indication of faculty response, the faculty role was mixed. In some instances, the faculty as a whole engaged in some sort of collective action designed to support their fired colleagues. Support ranged from writing letters to administrators and trustees protesting treatment of the dismissed faculty member to participating in the organization of an informal caucus or even a union. In other cases, faculty members pursued formation of an advisory body with a national support organization, such as an AAUP chapter, as a collective approach to problems with the administration.

The AAUP deals with institutions that deny faculty members a voice in governance in the same way that it treats other violations of academic freedom. The AAUP carefully investigates the charges against the institution and, if the investigating committee finds against the institution, the AAUP places the institution on a censure list that is published nationally. The AAUP then works with the censured administrations to develop personnel policies and governance practices that give faculty a voice in institutional decisions. Over the course of twenty years, fourteen (48 percent) of the twenty-nine institutions eventually complied with AAUP guidelines.

Some faculty, who lacked an adequate role in academic governance, turned to collective bargaining. Theoretically, as organizations become larger the bargaining power of individuals decreases; therefore collective negotiation, which strengthens the position of an atomized labor force, is used to achieve fairer and more equitable contracts. Large numbers of faculty have unionized. As of 1993, 35.7 percent of community college faculty and 27.5 percent of four-year faculty were unionized (Douglas and Or, 1993). However, faculty at private sector institutions were largely precluded from bargaining due to the Yeshiva decision. Moreover, even unionized faculty members have been unable to negotiate contracts that give them much direct protection against job loss during retrenchment (Rhoades, 1993).

Faculty are sometimes able to achieve results by turning to the courts. Frequently they have been defeated at the local level but have been able to win at appellate levels. For example, a faculty member at Husson College in Maine and some of the faculty at Alabama State University won court cases, and faculty members in the Virginia Community College system resolved their problems over job security in the courts. However, appealing verdicts is costly and time-consuming. Institutions have an advantage because they usually have much deeper pockets than faculty members. Moreover, although court decisions have compensated individuals, they have not necessarily empowered faculties as a collectivity.

When the courts have attempted to deal with the governance rights of faculty members as a collectivity, their treatment has been ambiguous. The Yeshiva decision says that faculty at private institutions do not have the right to bargain collectively because they have professional rights and duties that make them more akin to managers than employees. However, faculty at some private institutions are not able to avail themselves of the professional rights and duties Yeshiva implies they have, leaving them with no way to counter the imbalance of power between themselves and the administration.

Although faculty members have been able to avail themselves of a variety of measures—the AAUP, union organization, the courts—to win the right to participate in institutional decision making and have sometimes been able to use these resources to check the power of their administrations, none of these remedies provide an easy solution to their problems.

Conclusion

Overall, the institutions at which dirty little cases have occurred are characterized by imbalances in power between administrators and faculty. The faculty at these institutions are by and large not cosmopolitan, not in strong market positions, and not connected to federal mission agencies or other external groups that might give them leverage in negotiating with their administrations. These faculty do not have access to power bases independent of their institutions in ways that faculty at elite institutions do.

Professionalization theories tend not to deal with these disparities in power within the profession. Trait theorists of professionalization tend not to take the institution of employment into account. Instead, the focus is on the individual professional. Individuals are responsible for acquiring the requisite badges of professional status—the proper credentials, publication of scholarly papers, participation in learned and professional associations, service to the community—and once a sufficient number of these are collected, they will be treated as professionals regardless of the type of institution at which they are employed (Etzioni, 1969; Clark, 1987).

Process theorists of professionalization are concerned with power relations, including those between professionals and the bureaucratic institutions that employ them. However, process theorists tend to build their theories on the histories of elite institutions, and they spend little time dealing with undistinguished four-year institutions or community colleges. Because of their focus on elite institutions, process theories of professionalization fail to analyze the faculty-administration dynamics that characterize non-elite institutions, by far the largest number of postsecondary institutions.

Despite process theorists' concentration on elite institutions, they perform an important service for faculty at non-elite institutions by illuminating the history of complex negotiations and compromises that faculty at elite institutions have made with administrations in an effort to maintain autonomy and secure rights to self-governance. Process theorists point to the array of power bases available to faculty at elite institutions: for example, positions in associations of learned disciplines; access to external sources of power and status, such as national and international prizes and honors; access to federal and foundation grants, to consulting opportunities, and to opportunities to create spin-off companies (Caplow and McGee, 1958; Jencks and Reisman, 1968; Kerr, 1963; Silva and Slaughter, 1984). Without these external power bases, faculty members at elite institutions might not have been able to gain an institutional voice, because they would have had no leverage in their negotiations with administrators.

Unless faculty at institutions that give rise to dirty little cases realize that access to multiple power bases are central to maintenance of faculty self-governance and academic freedom, they will not be able to make a realistic assessment of the odds they face when they attempt to gain recognition as professionals. Although unionization is a characteristic that trait theorists often see as a counterindication of professional status, some form of collective action that draws on the power of state and national non-governmental organizations might serve these professors better than intrainstitutional appeals to administrators to recognize their professional stature. Not coincidentally, community colleges are the most highly unionized sector and four-year colleges are next. Faculty at institutions in these sectors have often found it necessary to turn to unionization to redress institutional imbalances in power and to give faculty members a voice administrators are compelled to listen to. However, as pointed out earlier, establishment of collective bargaining has become more difficult, as have negotiations with administrators under existing collective bargaining agreements.

Neither trait nor process theories of professionalization tend to explore internal institutional conflict surrounding efforts of faculty members to gain rights to self-governance—trait theorists because they do not see professionalization as characterized by power struggles, and process theorists because the professionals on whom they concentrate usually have strong negotiating positions with their administrations. This lack of attention to prolonged periods of intense intrainstitutional conflict over professorial autonomy and governance rights leaves faculty members unprepared for the length and viciousness that is often characteristic of struggles for self-governance. The dirty little cases studied often went on for years, polarizing the faculty into rigid factions, locking faculty and administrators into adversarial relations, making everyday discourse almost impossible. This breakdown of the academic community undoubtedly adversely affected the collaborative exchanges necessary to the education of students and the production of scholarship.

Given that the vast majority of two- and four-year institutions do *not* give rise to dirty little cases—apparently honoring tenure, academic freedom, and faculty self-governance rights—and that urbanization is increasing and the South has in many ways been incorporated in national professional communities, it is tempting to assume that dirty little cases will gradually disappear as all institutions will come to honor professional norms that provide faculty with an authentic voice in governance. However, several factors suggest that these cases are unlikely to diminish. First, as noted earlier, they are not currently decreasing; they remain the most regular of all academic freedom cases reported by the AAUP. Second, the broad restructuring of postsecondary education presently taking place usually involves curtailment, if not temporary elimination, of professors' participation in governance. Third, the legal and customary structures—such as tenure—that have protected professors who raised their voices on institutional issues are increasingly challenged by a conservative national political climate that values management's voice above all others.

Academic freedom, and particularly the faculty's institutional voice as expressed in governance, is important for all colleges and universities. To limit an authentic voice in institutional governance to faculty at elite institutions does a disservice not only to faculty but to administrators as well. In a period of academic restructuring such as we currently face, faculty are the group that know more about instructional delivery and production of scholarship than any other. They, more than any other group, should be able to contribute their expertise to a discussion of how to change higher education.

Notes

1. The phrase "dirty little cases" was coined by Jordan Kurland, longtime staff to the American Association of University Professors (AAUP) Committee A (Academic Freedom) (Jordan Kurland, interview with author, 1980).
2. For purposes of this analysis, I combined categories that were separate in earlier articles (1987, 1994) I wrote using the same data set. In this chapter, the categories of political action, religious action, and civil liberties are combined into a single category dealing with freedom of speech and action.
3. The literature on prestige and status in postsecondary education usually views prestige and status in terms of hierarchy, function, and characteristics of the student body and the faculty. Although analytically separate, place in hierarchy and function tend to coincide. In many ways, place in hierarchy is determined by years of education. Thus community colleges, which provide two years of education, are at the bottom. In terms of function, they provide remedial education, technical education, and basic courses for transfer to four-year institutions, all of which are usually regarded as less complex than what occurs at four-year institutions. Research universities are usually at the top of the hierarchy, and graduate education and scholarship are regarded as more complex than undergraduate teaching. When all institutions are located in a similar sector in the hierarchy (community college, four-year liberal arts, comprehensive university, and so on), the characteristics of students and faculty tend to determine which four-year liberal arts school, for example, has higher status and prestige. For example, four-year schools that have students with high SAT scores, high grade point averages, and National Merit scholars or holders of other scholarships are regarded as prestigious. Graduate schools with faculty who bring in large amounts of research monies, win Nobel prizes, and publish widely are regarded as high in status.

References

Caplow, T., and McGee, R. J. *The Academic Marketplace.* New York: Basic Books, 1958.
Carnegie Commission on Higher Education. *A Classification of Institutions of Higher Education.* Princeton, N.J.: Carnegie Foundation for the Advancement of Teaching, 1973.
Carnegie Commission on Higher Education. *A Classification of Institutions of Higher Education.* (Rev. ed.) Princeton, N.J.: Carnegie Foundation for the Advancement of Teaching, 1987.
Clark, B. R. *The Academic Life: Small Worlds.* Princeton, N.J.: Carnegie Foundation for the Advancement of Teaching, 1987.
Committee A. "Academic Freedom and Tenure: Laredo Junior College (Texas)." *American Association of University Professors Bulletin,* 1970, 56 (4), 398–404.
Committee A. "Academic Freedom and Tenure: Illinois College of Optometry." *Academe,* 1982, 68 (Nov.-Dec.), 17a–23a.
Committee A. "Academic Freedom and Tenure: University of Northern Colorado." *Academe,* 1984, 70 (May-June), 1a–8a.
Committee A. "Academic Freedom and Tenure: University of Northern Colorado. A Supplementary Report on a Censured Administration." *Academe,* 1986a, 71 (July-Aug.), 2a–4a.
Committee A. "Academic Freedom and Tenure: Talladega College (Alabama)." *Academe,* 1986b, 72 (May-June).
Committee A. "Academic Freedom and Tenure: Hillsdale College (Michigan)." *Academe,* 1988, 75 (May-June), 29–34.
Committee A. "Academic Freedom and Tenure: Alvernia College (Pennsylvania)." *Academe,* Jan.-Feb. 1990, pp. 67–74.
Douglas, J. M., and Or, B. G. *Directory of Faculty Contracts and Bargaining Agents in Institutions of Higher Education.* Vol. 16. New York: National Center for the Study of Collective Bargaining in Higher Education and the Professions, Baruch College, City University of New York, 1993.
Etzioni, A. (ed.) *The Semi-Professions and their Organization: Teachers, Nurses and Social Workers.* New York: Free Press, 1969.
Friedson, E. *Professional Powers: A Study of the Institutionalization of Formal Knowledge.* Chicago: University of Chicago Press, 1986.
Gouldner, A. W. "Locals and Cosmopolitans." *Administrative Science Quarterly,* 1957, 1, 281–306, 444–480.
Greenwood, E. "Attributes of a Profession." *Social Work,* 1957, 2 (April), 44–55.
Jencks, C., and Reisman, D. *The Academic Revolution.* New York: Doubleday, 1968.
Kerr, C. *The Uses of the University.* Cambridge, Mass.: Harvard University Press, 1963.
Larson, M. S. *The Rise of Professionalism: A Sociological Analysis.* Berkeley: University of California Press, 1977.
Moore, W. E. *The Professions: Roles and Rules.* New York: Russell Sage Foundation, 1970.
National Labor Relations Board v. Yeshiva University [444 U.S. 672 (1980)].
Rhoades, G. "Retrenchment Clauses in Faculty Union Contracts: Faculty Rights and Administrative Discretion." *Journal of Higher Education,* 1993, 64, 312–347.
Silva, E. T., and Slaughter, S. *Serving Power: The Making of the American Social Science Expert.* Westport, Conn.: Greenwood, 1984.
Slaughter, S. "The Danger Zone: Academic Freedom and Civil Liberties." *Annals of the American Academy of Political and Social Science,* 1980, 448 (March), 781–819.
Slaughter, S. "Academic Freedom in the Modern University." In P. G. Altbach and R. O. Berdahl (eds.), *Higher Education in American Society.* (Rev. ed.). Buffalo, N.Y.: Prometheus, 1987.
Slaughter, S. (ed.). *Journal of Higher Education,* 1993a, 64 (entire May-June issue). (Special issue on retrenchment.)
Slaughter, S. "Retrenchment in the 1980s: The Politics of Prestige and Gender." *Journal of Higher Education,* 1993b, 64 (May-June), 250–282.

Slaughter, S. "Academic Freedom in the 1980s: Decomposition of Professional Labor, Patterns of Gender Preference and Problems with Faculty Professionalization." In P. G. Altbach, R. O. Berdahl, and P. Gumport (eds.), *Higher Education in American Society.* (3rd ed.) Buffalo, N.Y.: Prometheus Books, in press.

Smith, M.L.A. *A Study of the Status of Tenure in the Nation's Public Two Year Colleges.* San Marcos: Southwest Texas University, 1984.

SHEILA SLAUGHTER *is professor of higher education at the University of Arizona at Tucson's Center for the Study of Higher Education. She is currently a fellow at the University of Arizona's Udall Policy Institute.*

The sphere of academic freedom is not equivalent to that of freedom of expression, but derives from and is limited to faculty professional responsibilities, including participation in academic governance.

Academic Freedom, Professionalism, and Intramural Speech

David M. Rabban

Definitions of academic freedom generally focus on the need to safeguard the intellectual independence of professors in research and teaching. Yet American universities in the twentieth century have only rarely attempted to punish professors for their scholarly ideas. Professors more commonly have been at greatest risk of discipline for speaking either about political issues beyond the campus or about university matters outside their scholarly expertise. Some commentators have addressed the relationship between academic freedom and political speech, but the application of academic freedom to intramural speech about university affairs has remained largely unexplored. I suggest in this essay that the more directly intramural speech relates to the professional function of the faculty in advancing knowledge and critical inquiry, the more it should be protected by academic freedom. Under this approach, a significant amount of intramural speech should be covered by academic freedom. But other intramural speech, including speech that should be protected by general theories applicable to all citizens and employees, is insufficiently related to professional concerns to justify the distinctive coverage of academic freedom.

The Range of Routine Disputes Involving Intramural Speech

Reports of investigating committees under the auspices of the American Association of University Professors (AAUP), as well as decisions in legal cases, reveal the range of routine disputes prompted by intramural speech. Many such disputes have related directly to research and teaching without implicating the content of the professor's scholarly ideas. Examples include the elimination of professional development funds (Wesley College, 1992, p. 24), policies on office hours (Claflin College, 1988, p. 41) and teaching loads (Wesley College, 1992, p. 24; Onondaga Community College, 1971, p. 174), administrative interference with faculty grading of students (College of Osteopathic Medicine and Surgery, 1977, p. 85), the manner of assigning teachers to courses (*Ballard v. Blount,* 1983, p. 162; *Dorsett v. Board of Trustees,* 1991, p. 123), and the imposition of a freshman English syllabus that "restricted a teacher's latitude in conducting the class" (*Ballard v. Blount,* 1983, p. 162). Faculty speech about other working conditions has provoked additional controversies. Professors have complained about salaries (*Ayoub v. Texas A & M University,* 1991, p. 837; *Ballard v. Blount,* 1983, p. 162; College of Osteopathic Medicine and Surgery, 1977, p. 85; Elmira College, 1993, p. 48; *Kurtz v. Vickrey,* 1988, p. 728; Talladega College, 1986, p. 6a), inadequate parking (Claflin College, 1988, p. 41), and the reduction of health care benefits for all university employees (Wesley College, 1992, p. 24).

Disputes over intramural speech have extended beyond a professor's immediate working conditions. Faculty members have protested the unilateral implementation of new policies that undermined tenure (Onondaga Community College, 1971, pp. 168, 173), the denial of tenure or reappointment to colleagues (*Ballard v. Blount,* 1983, p. 162; North Greenville College, 1993, p. 63), and the renewal of another professor's appointment (*Narumanchi v. Board of Trustees,* 1988, p. 73). In addition to expressing concerns related directly to faculty status, professors have complained about inadequate faculty governance when universities promulgated a new faculty handbook without faculty participation (Lees College, 1993, p. 50), refused to establish a faculty senate (Lees College, 1993, p. 50), and replaced faculty senates with "meet and confer" sessions dominated by the newly elected faculty union (*Minnesota State Board for Community Colleges v. Knight,* 1984).

Broader issues of educational policy have generated controversial intramural speech. Professors have made recommendations about the curriculum (*Landrum v. Eastern Kentucky University,* 1984, p. 244), such as reforms designed to include the multicultural perspectives of minorities (*Jeffries v. Harleston,* 1993, pp. 742–743). Other professors have opposed the administration's imposition of a curriculum on the faculty (College of Osteopathic Medicine and Surgery, p. 85). Faculty members have similarly protested their exclusion from decisions about departmental reorganization (Mount Ida College, 1984, p. 42a; *Narumanchi v. Board of Trustees,* 1988, pp. 72–73; Talladega College, 1986, p. 8a). A professor dismissed after advocating the transformation of a junior college to a four-year institution, a position opposed by the college's board of regents, brought a lawsuit ultimately decided by the United States Supreme Court (*Perry v. Sindermann,* 1972).

Faculty have also raised concerns about academic standards. While agreeing that her college had a special mission to educate poorly prepared students, a professor warned against lowering standards in the process (Claflin College, 1988, pp. 46, 47). Other professors have urged higher admissions standards for students (North Greenville College, 1993, p. 58), protested grade inflation (*Dorsett v. Board of Trustees,* 1991, p. 124; *Johnson v. Lincoln University,* 1985, p. 452), castigated colleagues for allowing students who had not passed prerequisites to take advanced courses (*Johnson v. Lincoln University,* 1985, p. 453), and written letters about a college's low academic standards to its accrediting association (p. 451).

Budgetary as well as academic issues have provoked faculty criticism of universities. Professors have protested their exclusion from deliberations that led to cuts in the university's budget (Wesley College, 1992, p. 25), criticized budgetary allocations by the administration (North Greenville College, 1993, p. 58; Talladega College, 1986, p. 6a), and attacked administrators for financial mismanagement (*Kurtz v. Vickrey,* 1988, p. 730). Specific comments sometimes related budgetary to educational matters. One professor, for example, protested that his university spent too much money on "window dressing" for the physical plant, but not enough for educational purposes (pp. 725, 729–730).

Other criticisms by professors against administrators have not involved academic issues. Professors have accused administrators of unethical or illegal activities involving financial misconduct (*Idoux v. Lamar University System,* 1993, pp. 1256–1257; Philander Smith College, 1980, p. 199), procurement of materials for the library (*Leachman v. Rector & Visitors,* 1988, p. 962), and alcohol policies (*Idoux v. Lamar University System,* 1993, p. 1256). Faculty have protested administrative bloat (Onondaga Community College, 1971, p. 174), the deplorable state of the university's physical plant (Onondaga Community College, 1971, p. 174), lack of presidential leadership in fund-raising (Wesley College, 1992, p. 27), and the board's choice of a new president (North Greenville College, 1993, p. 63). Intramural speech has extended to campus disputes touching on broad social issues. In a case that reached the United States Supreme Court, for example, a professor publicly criticized the administration for suspending a large group of black students without determining individual guilt (*Board of Regents v. Roth,* 1972, p. 579).

Does the Traditional Justification for Academic Freedom Apply to Intramural Speech?

The traditional American justification for academic freedom, which derives from the AAUP's 1915 declaration, does not apply easily to these many examples of intramural speech on university affairs. The 1915 declaration emphasized that academic freedom allows professors to serve society by using their specialized expertise to advance knowledge. Professors should have "freedom to perform honestly and according to their own consciences the distinctive and important function which the nature of the profession lays upon them." "That function," the declaration continued, "is to deal at first hand, after prolonged and specialized technical training, with the sources of knowledge; and to impart the results of their own and of their fellow specialists' investigation and reflection, both to students and to the general public, without fear or favor." Academic freedom benefits the society at large because it helps ensure "that what purport to be the conclusions of men trained for, and dedicated to, the quest for truth, shall in fact be the conclusions of such men, and not echoes of the opinions of the lay public, or of the individuals who endow or manage universities" (AAUP, 1969, p. 162). Because the "scholar has professional functions to perform in which the appointing authorities have neither competency nor moral right to intervene" (p. 165), the declaration added, professors should not be treated as mere employees of university trustees.

To what extent does this justification for academic freedom in the "professional functions" of the scholar extend to speech outside the professor's own academic discipline? The 1915 declaration identified three elements of academic freedom: "freedom of inquiry and research; freedom of teaching within the university or college; and freedom of extramural utterance and action" (p. 158). In elaborating the meaning of extramural utterance, the 1915 declaration stressed that while a professor has "a peculiar obligation to avoid hasty or unverified or exaggerated statements, and to refrain from intemperate or sensational modes of expression," it is not "desirable that scholars should be debarred from giving expression to their judgments upon controversial questions, or that their freedom of speech, outside the university, should be limited to questions falling within their own specialties" (p. 172). The 1915 declaration did not specifically address the relationship of academic freedom to intramural speech on university affairs. Yet if faculty members have academic freedom to speak as citizens about political issues having nothing to do with the university, one could easily maintain that they should be able to speak about university matters beyond their narrow disciplinary concerns.

The extension of academic freedom to speech outside the specialized competence of professors, however, was controversial even within the AAUP. The committee that drafted the 1915 declaration initially worried that "academic freedom would lose its rationale if it were stretched to protect activities not performed in the course of professional duty" (Metzger, 1988, p. 1274). Recent commentators on academic freedom have revived this concern. In an influential article, William Van Alstyne objected to the "promiscuous" extension of academic freedom from "a close association with protection of the academic in his professional endeavors" to the "general civil liberties of academics" (Van Alstyne, 1975, pp. 60, 62; see also Byrne, 1989, and Rabban, 1990).

To a substantial extent, historical factors account for the application of academic freedom beyond purely professional concerns. The 1915 declaration observed in its opening paragraph that all five of the cases investigated during the first year of the AAUP's existence "have involved, at least as one factor, the right of university teachers to express their opinions freely outside the university or to engage in political activities in their capacity as citizens" (p. 158). After stating that the declaration would deal primarily with "freedom of teaching within the university," its framers assumed without further explanation that the same principles are "also applicable to the freedom of speech of university teachers outside their institutions" (p. 158).

Although the pragmatic need to protect the extramural speech of professors may explain the broad application of academic freedom by the 1915 declaration, commentators have offered more theoretical arguments that would also cover intramural speech on university affairs. Some assert that professors should be entitled "not to suffer academic penalties through the exercise of their rights as citizens" (Searle, 1972, p. 94). Others point out that the line between professional and nonprofessional speech is often hard to draw (Rorty, 1972, p. 98). They worry that limiting academic freedom to speech within a professor's specialized expertise would have a "chilling effect" and would deter even professional speech that might be close to this line (Finkin, 1988, pp. 1342–1343). They also warn that a narrow conception of academic freedom would encourage autocratic administrators to use unprotected, nonprofessional speech as a pretext for termination when the real reason is the professor's controversial scholarly ideas (Finkin, 1988, pp. 1344–1345).

I do not find these arguments convincing. As a preliminary matter, it is important to dissociate the desirability of protecting the speech of professors from the more specific issue of whether the theory of academic freedom is the appropriate vehicle. Many commentators apparently assume that the free speech of professors depends entirely on their academic freedom. But professors can justify their exercise of free speech on other grounds. Professors, like all citizens, should have the right to comment on public affairs; similarly, they should have the right, like all employees, to comment on working conditions and employer policies. To some extent, these rights are protected by the First Amendment and by university grievance procedures. Good arguments can be made that professors, like other citizens and workers, should have more free speech than they currently enjoy. But unless these arguments derive from the "professional functions" of the scholar in critical inquiry, they cannot convincingly be justified by the concept of academic freedom. Attempts to extend academic freedom beyond professional speech raise the legitimate complaint of special pleading by professors for rights to which they are no more entitled than anyone else.

Penalizing professors for nonprofessional speech, however, can affect their professional functions. Faculty members who express unpopular political or personal views may be more likely to express controversial scholarly ideas as well. Even if no such correlation exists, professors disciplined or discharged for nonprofessional speech may include brilliant teachers and scholars. Yet this impact on professional speech seems too speculative and indirect to warrant the coverage of academic freedom.

More closely connected to the justification for academic freedom are concerns that a distinction between professional and nonprofessional speech would not adequately protect professional speech. The category of nonprofessional speech, as commentators have argued (see Finkin, 1988), could "chill" or serve as a pretext for punishing speech that should be considered professional. On the other hand, much nonprofessional speech by faculty is clearly unrelated to professional concerns, and the danger of pretextual abuse is uncertain and perhaps exaggerated. Broadening academic freedom to cover all speech by professors runs the risk of diluting its conceptual power to safeguard the core professional functions of a scholar. Instead of stretching the definition of academic freedom, a term that provides unique benefits to a single profession, beyond its most convincing justification, it makes more pragmatic and theoretical sense to encourage a generous definition of professional speech.

Defining the Professional Functions of a Scholar

Do the professional functions of a scholar that merit the protection of academic freedom include intramural speech on university affairs? Some administrators assert not, even as they reiterate their commitment to academic freedom in teaching and research (North Greenville College, 1993, pp. 54, 56; Wesley College, 1992, p. 33, 34 n. 2). The 1915 declaration and other commentary provide some support for their position by grounding the defense of academic freedom in the public benefit from the independent search for knowledge by trained specialists. This work is overwhelmingly performed through research and teaching, and much intramural speech does not flow from disciplinary expertise. Yet convincing arguments support a conception of academic freedom that protects a substantial amount of intramural speech.

The 1915 declaration itself, while emphasizing the social benefits of research and teaching, also made some incipient connections between academic freedom and peer review. The same expertise that justifies academic freedom, the declaration asserted, places on professors the correlative obligation to determine if their colleagues have departed "from the requirements of the scientific spirit and method." Because bodies not composed of professors "necessarily lack full competency to judge" this professional issue, "their intervention can never be exempt from the suspicion that it is dictated by other motives than zeal for the integrity of science" (p. 169).

The "practical proposals" appended to the 1915 declaration elaborated the connection between academic freedom and peer review. The first proposal urged that universities provide "suitable judicial bodies, composed of members of the academic profession, which may be called into action before university teachers are dismissed or disciplined, and may determine in what cases the question of academic freedom is actually involved." The proposals also maintained that faculty committees should advise before universities decide whether or not to reappoint professors (p. 174).

The 1915 declaration thus conceived of peer review as a necessary structural support of academic freedom. For peer review to operate effectively, faculty participants must be free to express their views on the professional merits of colleagues. Such expression should constitute part of the "professional functions" of a scholar protected by academic freedom.

Analogous arguments can be made for extending academic freedom to intramural speech by faculty while they are performing their professional functions in other matters of university governance. The 1966 "Statement on Government of Colleges and Universities," jointly formulated by the AAUP, the

American Council on Education, and the Association of Governing Boards of Universities and Colleges, elaborated the division and sharing of authority in universities. Emphasizing that faculty "judgment is central to general educational policy," the 1966 statement declared that the "faculty has primary responsibility for such fundamental areas as curriculum, subject matter and methods of instruction, research, faculty status, and those aspects of student life which relate to the educational process" (p. 123). All members of the United States Supreme Court reached a similar conclusion, even while vigorously disagreeing about whether this responsibility defines faculty as managers under the National Labor Relations Act. Universities require "faculty participation in governance," the majority observed in *National Labor Relations Board v. Yeshiva University* (1980) "because professional expertise is indispensable to the formulation and implementation of academic policy" (p. 689).

In contrast to the explicit connection between peer review and academic freedom in the 1915 declaration, neither the 1966 statement nor the Supreme Court majority in the Yeshiva case linked the faculty's "primary" and "indispensable" professional role in educational governance directly to academic freedom. This link, however, is not hard to establish. Faculty expertise contributes to the critical search for knowledge that justifies academic freedom—not just through teaching and research, but also through the broader determination of educational policies on curriculum, the organization of academic departments, academic standards, the educational implications of budgetary decisions, and many other subjects of recurring disputes revealed by AAUP reports and legal decisions.

Interestingly, legal decisions provide more support for a connection between faculty speech on educational policy and academic freedom than does AAUP policy. The 1966 statement recognized a right "to speak on general educational questions or about the administration and operations of the individual's own institution." Yet the statement, rather than relying on the professional functions of the faculty protected by academic freedom, identified this right in a section on "external relations of the institution" and extended it to all members of the university community in their role as citizens (pp. 121–122).

A footnote reinforces this point by quoting the "1940 Statement of Principles on Academic Freedom and Tenure," a document formulated by the AAUP and the Association of American Colleges, endorsed by over 150 educational organizations, and frequently relied on by courts in construing the contractual rights of faculty members. According to the portion of the 1940 statement quoted in the footnote, when faculty "speak or write as citizens, they should be free from institutional censorship or discipline," but as scholars and "officers of an educational institution" they should recognize that "their special position in the community imposes special obligations" to "exercise appropriate restraint" (p. 122, n. 2). Reports of AAUP investigating committees frequently claim that faculty, in their role as educational officers, must have academic freedom to discuss intramural affairs (Claflin College, 1988, p. 45; Elmira College, 1993, p. 49; Mount Ida College, 1984, p. 41a; Talladega

College, 1986, p. 13a). The quoted language, however, makes clear that the 1940 and 1966 statements invoked this role not to justify intramural speech by faculty as part of their professional functions, but to circumscribe faculty speech as citizens in connection with an unconvincing conception of academic freedom that includes nonprofessional speech.

Some opinions by United States Supreme Court justices, by contrast, more closely relate the faculty's professional responsibilities for educational policy to academic freedom. The majority in the Yeshiva case, without specifically mentioning academic freedom, acknowledged the "large measure of independence enjoyed by faculty" in academic governance (pp. 689–690). The dissenting opinion went further and specifically attributed this independence to the protection academic freedom affords "a faculty member's professional competence" (p. 700). In upholding a faculty committee's decision that prohibited a medical student from retaking an important examination, a unanimous Supreme Court more directly connected academic freedom to the faculty's role in determining educational policy. Writing for a unanimous court, Justice Stevens relied on prior cases incorporating academic freedom within the First Amendment to emphasize that judges "asked to review the substance of a genuinely academic decision . . . should show great respect for the faculty's professional judgment" (*Regents of University of Michigan v. Ewing*, 1985, p. 225). Although a Supreme Court majority in another case refused to interpret the constitutional definition of academic freedom as requiring universities to establish structures for faculty participation in governance, all three opinions in the case stressed that the First Amendment protects the right of professors to express their views on matters of educational policy (*Minnesota State Board for Community Colleges v. Knight*, 1984).

Much intramural speech by professors, however, does not address educational policy. As citizens, faculty should be able to report illegal activities on campus that have nothing to do with educational policies. As employees, they should be able to complain about their wages and benefits and about perceived weaknesses in the performance of nonacademic functions by administrators and governing boards. But protection for such intramural speech, like protection for speech on external political affairs outside a professor's disciplinary expertise, cannot derive from a convincing theory of academic freedom. Nor should academic freedom cover faculty speech, even on educational matters, that deviates substantially from reasonable standards of civility. Speech that disrupts classes or meetings, is laced with profanity or abusive personal invective, discloses legitimately confidential information, or is false or libelous may provide grounds for discipline.

Bridging the Gap Between AAUP Policy and Legal Doctrine

The relationship between academic freedom and intramural speech defended in this essay bridges some gaps in existing AAUP policy and in legal doctrine. The AAUP's two major policy documents on academic freedom, the 1915 declaration and the 1940 statement, do not refer to intramural speech, and its most comprehensive document on university government, the 1966 statement, does not refer to academic freedom. (A recent AAUP report, "On the Relationship of Faculty Governance to Academic Freedom" [1994, p. 47], has recognized that "the AAUP has not spoken explicitly to the links between its principles in these two basic areas." In remedying this deficiency, the report identifies "the academic freedom of faculty members in addressing issues of institutional governance" as "a prerequisite for the practice of governance unhampered by fear of retribution" [p. 47]. The report neither relates academic freedom on matters of institutional governance to the justification for academic freedom in the 1915 declaration nor explores intramural speech on other subjects.) Nevertheless, the public benefit from the search for knowledge by specialized experts, the primary justification for academic freedom by the AAUP, applies to intramural speech on educational policy.

The same justification for academic freedom, as several commentators have observed (Byrne, 1989; Rabban, 1990; Van Alstyne, 1975), could help the United States Supreme Court clarify the constitutional status of academic freedom. In striking contrast to its development of freedom of association as a distinctive concept under the First Amendment, the Court has not effectively differentiated its frequent reiterations of academic freedom as "a special concern of the First Amendment" (*Keyishian* v. *Board of Regents,* 1967, p. 603) from general First Amendment rights to free speech (Van Alstyne, 1975, pp. 66–67). As a result, the judiciary frequently has applied First Amendment principles to the university context without considering their possible impact on academic freedom.

In evaluating intramural speech, several courts have relied on *Connick* v. *Myers* (1983), an important Supreme Court decision holding that the First Amendment protects speech by public employees only on matters of "public concern." Under this analysis, courts have reached inconsistent conclusions about whether academic standards (*Dorsett* v. *Board of Trustees,* 1991, p. 124; *Johnson* v. *Lincoln University,* 1985, p. 452) and curriculum (*Ballard* v. *Blount,* 1983, p. 163; *Jeffries* v. *Harleston,* 1993, p. 743; *Landrum* v. *Eastern Kentucky University,* 1984, p. 244) are matters of public concern. One decision held that faculty protests over administrative decisions denying or granting tenure to colleagues cannot be characterized as a public concern (*Ballard* v. *Blount,* 1983, pp. 164–165). None of these cases mentioned special First Amendment protection for academic freedom.

As Justice Stevens has emphasized, however, constitutional academic freedom should protect the professional judgments of faculty on matters of educational policy (*Regents of University of Michigan* v. *Ewing,* 1985). Faculty speech on intramural affairs is an excellent example of an area in which a distinctive theory of academic freedom could lead to different results than a general theory of free speech (see Rabban, 1990; Van Alstyne, 1975). Intramural faculty speech about educational policy should be protected by First Amendment academic freedom even if it is not considered a matter of public concern under the general First Amendment test of the Connick case.

Conclusion

The proper scope of academic freedom should be distinguished from the appropriate protections for faculty speech. Faculty members share with other citizens and employees legitimate interests in speaking on matters related to government and employment. Academic freedom, however, is justified by the distinctive public benefit derived from the specialized expertise of professors in advancing knowledge and critical inquiry. Faculty speech unrelated to these professional functions is beyond the scope of academic freedom, even if it should be protected on other grounds.

The professional functions of faculty members are most evident in their research and teaching. But faculty members have additional functions as institutional citizens that contribute to the search for knowledge. AAUP reports and legal cases usefully illustrate the extent to which intramural speech about university affairs merits the coverage of academic freedom.

Speech by professors about faculty status and educational policy, subjects the "Statement on Government of Colleges and Universities" designates as the "primary responsibility" of the faculty, clearly draws on professional expertise to advance the search for knowledge. Academic freedom, therefore, should protect comments about tenure policy and decisions, the faculty role in institutional governance, curriculum, academic standards, and the many issues that influence a professor's ability to teach and conduct research, such as grading policies, determination of course syllabi, class size, teaching loads, and professional development funds. On the other hand, many comments about working conditions and administrative practices seem insufficiently related to the search for knowledge to merit the protection of academic freedom. Examples include complaints regarding inadequate salaries, parking, and health and pension benefits, and criticism of administrators and governing boards concerning fund-raising, investment policies, maintenance of the physical plant, unethical or illegal financial dealings, and excessive staffing for bureaucratic functions.

Distinctions between categories may produce difficult borderline cases. Faculty criticism of administrative financial decisions may include comments on their educational consequences, a point illustrated by the faculty member who protested that the university's spending on the physical plant left inadequate funds for educational purposes. Similarly, a faculty member might claim that he received an inconvenient parking space in retaliation for controversial positions he took on faculty appointments and curricular policy. I find it striking how few of the AAUP reports and legal cases involve such "mixed" situations. I am also confident that close cases can be fairly resolved by keeping firmly in mind the justification for academic freedom in the distinctive professional functions of faculty members and not in more general views about when faculty speech should be protected. In my opinion, the more academic freedom is confined to its convincing justification, the greater the probability that academic decision makers and judges will take seriously the implications for academic freedom in close cases.

References

American Association of University Professors (AAUP). "Declaration of Principles (1915)." In L. Joughin (ed.), *Academic Freedom and Tenure*. Madison: University of Wisconsin Press, 1969.
Ayoub v. Texas A & M University [927 F.2d 834 (5th Cir. 1991)].
Ballard v. Blount [581 F. Supp. 160 (N.D. Ga. 1983)].
Board of Regents v. Roth [408 U.S. 564 (1972)].
Byrne, P. "Academic Freedom: A 'Special Concern of the First Amendment.'" *Yale Law Journal*, 1989, 99, 251–340.
Claflin College (South Carolina). *Academe*, May–June 1988, p. 41.
College of Osteopathic Medicine and Surgery (Iowa). *AAUP Bulletin*, April 1977, p. 82.
Connick v. Myers [461 U.S. 138 (1983)].
Dorsett v. Board of Trustees [940 F.2d 121 (5th Cir. 1991)].
Elmira College (New York). *Academe*, Sept.–Oct. 1993, p. 42.
Finkin, M. W. "Intramural Speech, Academic Freedom, and the First Amendment." *Texas Law Review*, 1988, 66, 1323–1349.
Idoux v. Lamar University System [828 F. Supp. 1252 (E.D. Tex. 1993)].
Jeffries v. Harleston [820 F. Supp. 741 (S.D. N.Y. 1993)].
Johnson v. Lincoln University [776 F.2d 443 (3d Cir. 1985)].
Keyishian v. Board of Regents [385 U.S. 589 (1967)].
Kurtz v. Vickrey [855 F.2d 723 (11th Cir. 1988)].
Landrum v. Eastern Kentucky University [578 F. Supp. 241 (E.D. Ky. 1984)].
Leachman v. Rector & Visitors [691 F. Supp. 961 (W.D. Va. 1988)].
Lees College (Kentucky). *Academe*, Jan.–Feb. 1993, p. 43.
Metzger, W. P. "Profession and Constitution: Two Definitions of Academic Freedom in America." *Texas Law Review*, 1988, 66, 1265–1322.
Minnesota State Board for Community Colleges v. Knight [465 U.S. 271 (1984)].
Mount Ida College (Massachusetts). *Academe*, Sept.–Oct. 1984, p. 41a.
Narumanchi v. Board of Trustees [850 F.2d 70 (2d Cir. 1988)].
National Labor Relations Board v. Yeshiva University [144 U.S. 672 (1980)].
"1940 Statement of Principles on Academic Freedom and Tenure." In *AAUP Policy Documents and Reports*. Washington, D.C.: American Association of University Professors, 1990, pp. 3–10.
North Greenville College (South Carolina). *Academe*, May–June 1993, p. 54.
"On the Relationship of Faculty Governance to Academic Freedom." *Academe*, July–Aug. 1994, p. 47.
Onondaga Community College (New York). *AAUP Bulletin*, Summer 1971, p. 167.
Perry v. Sindermann [408 U.S. 593 (1972)].
Philander Smith College (Arkansas). *Academe*, May 1990, p. 198.
Rabban, D. M. "A Functional Analysis of 'Individual' and 'Institutional' Academic Freedom Under the First Amendment." *Law and Contemporary Problems*, 1990, 53, 227–301.
Regents of University of Michigan v. Ewing [474 U.S. 214 (1985)].
Rorty, A. O. "Dilemmas of Academic and Intellectual Freedom." In E. Pincoffs (ed.), *The Concept of Academic Freedom*. Austin: University of Texas Press, 1975.
Searle, J. R. "Two Concepts of Academic Freedom." In E. Pincoffs (ed.), *The Concept of Academic Freedom*. Austin: University of Texas Press, 1975.
"Statement on Government of Colleges and Universities." In *AAUP Policy Documents and Reports*. Washington, D.C.: American Association of University Professors, 1990.
Talladega College (Alabama). *Academe*, May–June 1986, p. 6a.
Van Alstyne, W. "The Specific Theory of Academic Freedom and the General Issue of Civil Liberty." In E. Pincoffs (ed.), *The Concept of Academic Freedom*. Austin: University of Texas Press, 1975.
Wesley College (Delaware). *Academe*, May–June 1992, p. 24.

DAVID M. RABBAN is Thomas Shelton Maxey Professor of Law at the University of Texas at Austin and former staff counsel to the American Association of University Professors.

Institutional self-evaluation and quality assurance through accreditation depend on and support academic freedom.

Academic Freedom and Regional Accreditation: Guarantors of Quality in the Academy

Sandra E. Elman

Current critiques of the academy, which have placed unusual strains on the relationship between accreditation and academic freedom, serve also to call our attention to the interdependence of accreditation and academic freedom. Some see accreditation as a means to encourage affirmative action and curricular diversity; others argue that accreditation should confine itself to ensuring traditional academic standards and should resist efforts to establish "politically correct" curricula. Many believe accreditation should ensure academic quality by establishing outcomes measures of student achievement; others fear that such measures may diminish the faculty autonomy and institutional diversity accreditation should protect. These debates not only demonstrate the currency and intensity of concern about academic freedom, but they also illuminate several facets of the complex relationship between academic freedom and accreditation.

The debate about the role of regional accreditation in ensuring institutional diversity sometimes turns on the question of whether accreditation should seek diversity *within* institutions or protect diversity *among* institutions. Proponents of interinstitutional diversity often argue that imposing diversity from without intrudes on institutional academic freedom; that is, the right of each institution to pursue its chosen mission through its distinctive curricula and community. Some also argue that imposing curricular diversity may circumscribe the freedom of individual faculty members to pursue their own best professional judgement. Proponents of intrainstitutional diversity argue, conversely, that diversity is essential to the academic freedom of individuals and groups within the institution; that is, that intrainstitutional diversity provides the essential ground to liberate teaching and learning from the confining conventions of a monolithic campus culture. Moreover, they argue that the vast majority of institutions, and especially prestigious and influential institutions, reflect the dominant culture and promote conformity rather than diversity. Each of these arguments assumes that accreditation should ensure academic freedom, each recognizes the importance of academic freedom, and each reflects a fear that academic freedom is in imminent danger.

The debate about the establishment, through the accreditation process, of student outcomes assessment also raises serious issues of institutional and individual academic freedom. Proponents argue that accreditation has a responsibility to ensure institutional quality and can meet this responsibility only by requiring that institutions assess student achievement. But, if outcomes measures are intended to provide assurance of relative institutional quality, then institutions must employ similar assessment instruments. Critics argue that standardized assessment instruments will threaten institutional autonomy by encouraging the adoption of common, examination-oriented curricula. Critics further argue that, within the institution, an assessment system may inappropriately infringe on the professional judgement of individual faculty members and the curricular objectives of individual students. This debate has intensified as the federal government has sought to employ accreditation guidelines as an instrument for regulating educational institutions.

Although the debates over diversity and outcomes assessment starkly illuminate the expectation that accreditation is responsible for the protection of academic freedom, they do not reflect a reciprocal and equally important aspect of the relationship between accreditation and academic freedom. Our system of accreditation is grounded in and depends upon academic freedom. Accreditation requires a system of professional peer review both within and among institutions. Although accreditation is formally a voluntary process, it is one on which federal financial aid and the value of student certification depend. Negative accreditation reviews may severely or fatally affect institutional survival. Nonetheless, administrators and faculty among and within institutions are expected to exercise their best, independent professional judgement in conducting reviews. Without a well-established foundation in academic freedom, it would be impossible to achieve the honest self-evaluation essential to the peer review system on which accreditation rests.

Accordingly, this article will focus on the reciprocal relationship between accreditation and academic freedom. On the one hand, it explores why and how accreditation considers academic freedom an integral component of institutional quality. On the other, it shows how academic freedom is critically necessary to facilitate the assurance of academic quality through the accreditation process. Both aspects of this reciprocal relationship will illuminate how and why academic freedom is an integral and essential basis for academic achievement.

Regional Accreditation and Institutional Mission

The regional accreditation process employs a clearly articulated set of criteria against which colleges and universities are evaluated—namely, standards for accreditation. These standards are generated by means of a consultative process involving all member institutions, and they are applied to the evaluation process by the respective commission in each region that deals with baccalaureate degree-granting and other, higher degree-granting institutions. To maintain accreditation, colleges and universities must demonstrate that these criteria have been adequately attained.

The accreditation process rests on the fundamental precept that the structures and programs of each institution are consistent with and serve to fulfill its stated mission and purposes. This provides the basis for an institutional evaluation. Regional accreditation associations mandate that an institution must have a mission and a set of purposes that are appropriate to higher education and that define its character in a manner consistent with the association's standards. Moreover, each institution must set forth a mission and purpose statement that "accurately delineates its character to the public it seeks to serve," thereby providing a basis for the evaluation of the institution against the commission's standards. These statements must be formally adopted by the institution's board of trustees. Institutions must demonstrate during the accreditation review that their mission and purpose statements are understood by the trustees, faculty, and administration; that they provide direction to the curricula; and that financial and physical resources allocation are clearly related to the mission (MSACS, 1990, pp. 9–11; NASC, 1992, pp. 27–28; NCACS, 1994, pp. 59–60; NEASC, 1992, p. 4; SACS, 1992, p. 13; WASC, 1988, p. 15).

Higher education commissions of regional accreditation bodies expect, therefore, that the goals and objectives of each college and university are concrete and realistic and define the educational and other dimensions of the institution, including teaching, research, public service, and other scholarly activities. In determining their mission, institutions must also define those aims and emphases that reflect their distinct character and individuality. Institutional mission statements both shape and reflect the campus culture. By periodically reevaluating the effectiveness of mission statements and ensuring that they are integrally linked to the prevailing culture, institutions enhance their capability to fulfill their mission and purposes. Faculty seek congruence between their institution's espoused mission, the norms and values of its culture, and their actual practices. Accreditation fosters this congruence (Elman, p. 72).

Accreditation Standards and Academic Freedom

Let us first review how the accreditation process views academic freedom. References to academic freedom in the various regional accreditation associations' standards are not only found, as would be expected, in their standards on faculty, but also in their standards on institutional integrity. This testifies to the fact that regional accreditation associations view academic freedom as integral to the life of an institution. Perhaps nowhere is the language on academic freedom in accreditation standards more compelling than in the Western Association of Schools and Colleges' (WASC) Standard on Institutional Integrity. Unambiguous in tone, the opening sentences of the first standard states that "an institution of higher education is, by definition, dedicated to the search for truth and its dissemination. As a consequence, faculty, students, administrators, trustees and staff are committed to and supported in the free pursuit of knowledge and the expression of ideas" (p. 9).

The Southern Association of Colleges and Schools (SACS), in its Standard on Educational Programs, and WASC, in its Standard on Institutional Integrity, employ identical language in stating that "the protection of the freedom for faculty and students to examine all pertinent data, to question assumptions, to be guided by the evidence of scholarly research, and to teach and study the substance of a given field is crucial to the integrity of an educational institution" (SACS, 1992, p. 42; WASC, 1988, p. 9). The New England Association of Schools and Colleges (NEASC), in its culminating Standard on Integrity, requires accredited institutions to adhere to these same criteria (p. 30).

The WASC standard goes on to profess that "there is no norm of greater value for educational institutions than academic freedom." Moreover, it continues, "political, social, religious, or philosophical beliefs may inform the curriculum, but must not restrict scholarly research, teaching and discussions" (p. 9). With equal resolve, the Middle States Association of Colleges and Schools' (MSACS) standards for accreditation proceed on the fundamental assumption that "appropriate autonomy and freedom" are essential conditions for ensuring "the maintenance and exercise of (such) institutional integrity" (p. 8). For the Northwest Association of Schools and Colleges' (NASC) Commission on Colleges, these very words are part of the guidelines that undergird its Policy on Institutional Integrity (NASC, p. 135). These notions of autonomy and freedom grow out of the fundamental assertion in NASC's policy that "by academic traditions and by philosophical principles, an institution of higher education is committed to the pursuit of truth and to its communication to others" (p. 135). The MSACS, in its first Standard on Institutional Integrity, concurs with NEASC and WASC in explaining what freedom involves, but it extends the notion by asserting that "autonomy is the freedom which allows an institution to get on with its essential work" (p. 8).

Academic freedom, then, does not just flourish without support, anymore than the grass on the campus green can grow without tending. As with all rights and liberties, its very existence rests upon the willingness of individuals to ensure its viability. Recognizing this dependence, the MSACS aptly points out that coupled with "intellectual and academic freedom" are "correlative responsibilities." This responsibility is shared. Trustees and administrators are obligated to provide leadership which "protect(s) all members of the institution from harassment or inappropriate measures." Faculty are obligated "to distinguish personal conviction from proven conclusions and to present relevant data fairly to students because this same freedom asserts their right to know the facts." Likewise, students are obligated "to sift and to question, to be involved actively in the life of the institution, but involved as learners at appropriate levels." And without question, "all concerned with the quality of educational institutions will seek ways to support their integrity and the exercise of their rightful autonomy and freedom" (MSACS, 1990, pp. 8–9).

Thus, individuals with various roles and of differing status within an institution are all obligated as members of the academy to bear the responsibility for ensuring that academic freedom is not compromised. For regional accreditation the protection of academic freedom is essential to ensuring not only the integrity of an institution but also, equally as important, its quality. Unquestionably, an institution's ability to exercise its "rightful autonomy and freedom" is viewed as the linchpin in optimizing the institution's quality and vitality (MSACS, 1990, p. 9).

Classroom and Curricula

Ordinarily the focus of academic freedom and its importance in the academy is centered on the classroom. That is, academic freedom is almost invariably associated with a faculty member's ability to engage in the teaching and learning process in a secure and protected environment. This notion is explicitly both an expectation and a goal of regional accreditation. In ensuring academic freedom, regional accreditation is concomitantly ensuring the quality of the academic enterprise. Thus, academic freedom facilitates the accomplishment of regional accreditation's goals.

Faculty concerns with respect to academic freedom center on the extent to which their rights as the conveyors of knowledge and their responsibilities as educators to develop the cognitive capabilities and intellect of their students are safeguarded by the institution. As such, academic freedom issues often surface in terms of the individual faculty member's relationship with his or her students in a classroom setting. Safeguarding this teaching relationship is of the utmost importance.

Nonetheless, there is another type of relationship in which academic freedom is essential. This type of relationship involves a faculty member not simply in his or her capacity as a teacher or academician, but rather as a member of the institution and the profession. Thus, the scope and complexity of the faculty member's role is multidimensional. Having an institutional affiliation implies the fulfillment of certain responsibilities. Over the last few decades, faculty have observed somewhat disenchantedly that their lives have become more stressful, in part because of ever-increasing demands on their time outside of the classroom. Yet, ironically, it is their very involvement in the institutional decision-making and planning processes that affords them the opportunity to have greater control over their fate in the classroom and within the institution.

Academic freedom is insufficiently recognized as a critical condition that makes possible an individual's role as an active participant in the life of an institution that is striving to meet its mission and purposes. Beyond the classroom, faculty are engaged in a variety of activities that contribute to the fulfillment of their institutions' educational objectives. As part of their responsibilities faculty are expected, in accordance with accreditation standards, to develop a curriculum of studies that offers students a substantial and coherent introduction to the broad areas of human knowledge as well as to their theories and methods of inquiry. All curricula must also provide an in-depth study in at least one disciplinary or interdisciplinary area (NEASC, 1992). Moreover, each undergraduate program at a regionally accredited institution must include a general education requirement that is coherent, substantive, and, in the words of the NEASC standards, "embodies the institution's definition of an educated person" (p. 11).

What satisfies that definition and accordingly constitutes various programs of study remains within the purview of each institution. The confluence of courses, bodies of knowledge, and intellectual experiences that a student needs to undergo in order to graduate as "an educated person" is, again, left to the discretion of each institution. Deliberations among faculty and administrators regarding curricula design are not without controversy. Invariably, such discussions (especially as of late) involve such polemical issues as how to address multiculturalism in the curriculum. For example, should all undergraduates or those majoring in certain fields be required to take courses in African history or Asian politics? Or should Western civilization be a mandatory, or even central, topic in the curriculum?

Faculty members are often steadfast in their intellectual commitment to a particular view on such matters. That these faculty are able to articulate and defend their views, irrespective of the fact that others disagree, is essential. Their willingness to propose and debate a course of action that is unpopular is predicated on the implicit understanding that it is legitimate to do so. Accreditation provides the leverage by which faculty may exercise their academic freedom, and disparate views on diversity can be deliberated and examined in an effort to make the wisest and most appropriate choice to achieve the institution's educational objectives and ensure academic excellence.

For the most part, accreditation criteria do not focus on what the conclusions should be with regard to issues such as diversity or multiculturalism. Rather, accreditation provides the means whereby the matter may be resolved collegially rather than by implicit or explicit pressure. Academic freedom, then, is crucial to ensuring that differing perspectives can be taken into account in developing curricular standards for specific majors and for various undergraduate programs overall.

Assessment: Determining Student Learning Outcomes

As government agencies and legislative bodies continue to question the efficiency and effectiveness of American higher education, the emphasis on assessment and student learning outcomes continues to gain increasing importance within as well as outside the academy. Over the last decade regional accreditation standards have addressed the issues of institutional effectiveness and assessment more explicitly and rigorously. Without exception, each regional accrediting association, in reviewing its standards, has reaffirmed and expanded the requirement that each institution measure its effectiveness. Accreditation associations regard an institution's efforts and ability to assess its own effectiveness and to utilize the resultant information for improvement as an important indicator of institutional quality.

"Assessment" has become a much-used and often abused term with various connotations which often elicit skeptical reactions from faculty and occasionally from administrators as well. In essence, the assessment process, according to NEASC, involves the collection and "analysis of evidence of congruence between an institution's stated mission, purposes and objectives and the actual outcomes of its programs and activities." Effective planning, decision making and resource allocation depends upon an institution's capability to create a culture of evidence by which it can determine how well and in what ways it is accomplishing its mission and purposes.

Recognizing the value and importance of honoring the "distinct character of each institution," NEASC, like its regional counterparts, embraces the notion that if the common goal of assessment and accreditation is to enable each institution to reach its "fullest academic potential by providing the highest quality education possible," then "institutional autonomy should be preserved and innovation encouraged." Innovation, though, does not just happen. It is the result of conscientious, introspective deliberations among colleagues—usually, though not exclusively, faculty members—in a climate that is conducive to risk taking and is characterized by a high level of trust. Assessment and innovation are inextricably linked insofar as developing meaningful ways to demonstrate student competencies and their knowledge base involves creating new mechanisms designed to tap a variety of concerns for a diverse population. Faculty throughout academe have been charged with this responsibility.

Accordingly, individual faculty members need to have the freedom and security to exercise their professional judgement regarding curriculum development, modes of delivery and instruction, academic advising, and precollegiate qualifications of students in order to undergo effective assessment. Of the various accreditation standards that address the issue of student competencies and hence the need for assessment, NEASC's Standard on Programs and Instruction best captures the rather daunting challenge that faculty confront: "Graduates successfully completing an undergraduate program demonstrate competence in written and oral communication in English; the ability for scientific and quantitative reasoning, for critical analysis and logical thinking; and the capability for continuing learning. They also demonstrate knowledge and understanding of scientific, historical, and social phenomena, and a knowledge and appreciation of the aesthetic and ethical dimensions of humankind. In addition, graduates demonstrate an in-depth understanding of an area of knowledge or practice and of its interrelatedness with other areas" (p. 12). Of foremost concern to faculty is not the formidable nature of such a challenge, but rather whether the need to formulate and implement assessment mechanisms will impose limits on the curriculum and impinge either upon faculty discretion in designing the curricula or on their method of instruction.

Assessment mechanisms need not only to reflect but also to be a direct outgrowth of the educational objectives of distinct departments. Just as faculty establish curricula jointly and produce joint texts, so too will they increasingly have to work together on formulating various means of assessment. More than ever, the challenge today is to establish mechanisms that on the one hand share commonalities but on the other hand embody the unique characteristics and aims of various programs of study. While it is reasonable to expect that assessment mechanisms should relate to the mission of the institution, it is difficult though not inconceivable to imagine implementing means of assessment that are applicable to *all* institutions. However, if common measures of student learning outcomes were to be imposed by external agencies such as the federal government, then faculty members would not have the latitude—that is, the academic freedom—to create innovative and tailored assessments that would capture the identified purpose and goals of their institution's educational programs. Accreditation, at least as we know it today, attempts to maintain a balance between mandating that institutions implement assessment activities and refraining from imposing specific, designated methods of assessment that would stifle faculty initiatives to develop qualitative and quantitative assessments that best reveal student performance.

Governance and Academic Freedom

While there can be little doubt that academic freedom is as integral to the life of the academy as the notion of free speech is to our democratic tradition, limits must be imposed or its utility can be diminished. The requirement that academic freedom be assured in an institution does not license faculty to decide every matter that arises within the institution. Faculty as a collectivity, and faculty members as individuals, are a prominent but not the sole authoritative constituency on campus. They play an important role in the organization and governance of the institution, but their role, like that of others, has to be defined in terms of the overall functioning and stability of the institution.

Here, again, regional accreditation provides a critical leverage point. While legislating the need for academic freedom to prevail at all colleges and universities, accreditation standards nevertheless must impose limits on academic freedom through required processes of governance. To ensure that institutions have in place a system of governance that facilitates the successful accomplishment of their respective mission and purposes, accreditation associations stipulate that "the authority, responsibilities, and relationships among the governing board, administration, staff and faculty are clearly described in a constitution, by laws or equivalent document, and in a table or organization that displays the actual working order of the institution." Moreover, accreditation standards expect the institution to demonstrate that "the board, administration, staff and faculty understand and fulfill their respective roles as set forth in the institution's official documents" (NEASC, 1992, p. 6).

In keeping with our democratic spirit of inclusion rather than exclusion, accreditation criteria require that the "institution's system of governance involves the participation of all appropriate constituencies and includes regular communication among them" (NEASC, 1992, p. 6). Accreditation standards clearly state the respective roles and responsibilities of institutions' governing board, their chief executive officer and administration, and their faculty. Intent on maintaining a level of institutional homeostasis (Thompson, 1967, p. 7) accreditation standards stipulate when it is appropriate for and expected that faculty will be active participants in the operation of an institution. NEASC's standards reflect the sentiment of their regional counterparts in maintaining that "the faculty assures the integrity of the institution's educational programs." Moreover, "within the context of the institution's system of governance, the faculty is accorded the right and exercises its responsibility to provide a substantive voice in matters of educational programs, faculty personnel, and other aspects of institutional policy that relate to its areas of responsibility and expertise" (p. 7). As such, through its designated processes of governance, accreditation assures a balance between providing faculty the opportunity to exercise their academic freedom and decision-making responsibility, wherever appropriate, and establishing parameters around those areas that are legitimately a part of their authoritative domain.

The Role of Academic Freedom in the Accreditation Process

Regional accreditation associations do not dictate specific course content nor which courses should be offered within a particular program of study. The role of regional accreditation is not to debate the appropriateness of the curriculum. Rather, accreditation seeks quality assurance through its periodic academic review. To ensure that educational programs have a "coherent design and are characterized by appropriate depth, breadth, continuity, sequential progression, and synthesis of learning," accreditation associations mandate that "as part of its overall planning and evaluation, the institution develops, approves, administers and periodically reviews its degree programs under established, clearly defined, and effective institutional policies which are demonstrably implemented by designated bodies with clearly established channels of communication and control." Such standards explicitly designate the faculty as those members of the institution having a "substantive responsibility" for the design, execution, and assessment of the curriculum (NEASC, 1992).

To assure faculty of this role in the accreditation process it is necessary to accord them the academic freedom to present their informed judgements without reprisal. A periodic systematic and comprehensive academic program review process, as required by regional accreditation associations, rests on the notion that recommendations to add or delete programs or courses are made after methodical analyses of their consistency with available resources, faculty expertise, student needs, and academic planning. Accreditation standards expect faculty members and others engaged in curricular planning and evaluation to take into account the role of the above-mentioned multiple resources required for the development and improvement of academic programs (NEASC, 1992, p. 9). During these review processes it is highly probable that contrasting perspectives will surface with regard to the status of all these variables. That faculty members are able to put forth their assessments of whether there is appropriate "faculty expertise" to sustain the academic quality of a given program or course presupposes that the tenets of academic freedom are upheld by all members of the institution's governing bodies.

Similar concerns apply with respect to regional accreditation requirements for planning and evaluation. For the most part, all the regional accrediting associations share NEASC's view that accredited institutions are expected to undertake planning and evaluation that is "broad-based, interrelated and appropriate to the institution's circumstances." Moreover, it is explicitly required that these processes "involve the participation of individuals and groups responsible for the achievement of institutional purposes." These individuals and groups are responsible for ensuring that, in undertaking both short- and long-term planning, the institution engages in "candid and realistic analyses of internal and external opportunities and constraints," and furthermore that "it responds to financial and other contingencies, establishes feasible priorities, and develops a realistic course of action to achieve identified objectives" (p. 5). That individuals, including faculty members, will articulate differing views of what constitutes "feasible priorities" and "a realistic course of action" during the course of planning and evaluation is expected; indeed, it is desirable if the institution is engaged in introspective self-examination and strives toward continuous improvement in accordance with regional accreditation policies and practices.

For faculty members to be active, involved, contributing members of these processes they must feel that they can articulate their views and defend what they see as a reasoned course of action irrespective of whether it is contrary to the view of a dean or an administrator who may serve on their tenure and promotion committee. Faculty members' security, and hence the quality of the participatory process, rests on the knowledge that the integrity of the process is protected by the principles of academic freedom, principles the institution embraces. Thus academic freedom serves to protect and ensure the dynamism and integrity of the planning and evaluation activities that are so integral to charting their institution's development and enhancing its overall educational quality.

Moreover, in many regions accreditation standards mandate that "the institution undertakes physical resource planning which is linked to academic and student services and financial planning." The NEASC's Standard on Physical Resources further stipulates that the "institution determines the adequacy of existing physical resources and identifies and plans the specified resolution of deferred maintenance needs" (NEASC, p. 25).

To achieve this end, it is necessary to involve those individuals, such as faculty members, who have firsthand knowledge of whether "the institution has sufficient and appropriate physical resources, including laboratories, materials, equipment, and buildings . . . [which] are designed, maintained, and managed at both on- and off-campus sites to serve institutional needs as defined by its mission and purposes" (NEASC, p. 25). Physical resource planning, like all types of planning, involves determining feasible priorities in light of financial constraints. Over the last decade, for example, colleges and universities have been confronted with the challenge of providing the state-of-the-art technology and equipment necessary for effectively delivering educational programs despite their having increasingly limited financial resources.

For faculty involvement to be meaningful and valuable in determining physical resources needs, faculty members need to know that their input, however critical it may be, will not be used against them in any punitive way. Moreover, faculty members need to feel that they have the right, indeed responsibility, to express concerns and make formal requests for what they perceive to be necessary equipment, materials, technology, and so forth to fulfill individual course and programmatic objectives, even if such requests are contrary to either particular administrators' or other faculty members' stances.

The essential role of academic freedom in accreditation and institutional planning complements the essential responsibility of accreditation for the assurance of academic freedom. This reciprocal relationship benefits institutions of higher education, their faculty and students, and the public they serve. Were government regulation substituted for voluntary accreditation, it would threaten the very foundation of academic freedom. Were academic freedom to atrophy, voluntary accreditation would cease to reflect honest and competent self-evaluation. The American system of voluntary accreditation is the essential complement to the American tradition of academic freedom.

References

Elman, S. E. "Regional Accreditation and the Evaluation of Faculty." *Metropolitan Universities,* 1994, 5 (1), 71–78.

Middle States Association of Colleges and Schools (MSACS), Commission on Higher Education. *Characteristics of Excellence in Higher Education.* (Rev. ed.) Philadelphia: Middle States Association of Colleges and Schools, 1990.

New England Association of Schools and Colleges (NEASC), Commission on Institutions of Higher Education. *Standards for Accreditation.* Winchester, Mass.: New England Association of Schools and Colleges, 1992.

North Central Association of Colleges and Schools (NCACS), Commission on Institutions of Higher Education. *A Handbook of Accreditation.* Chicago: North Central Association of Colleges and Schools, 1994.

Northwest Association of Schools and Colleges (NASC), Commission on Colleges. *Accreditation Handbook.* Seattle, Wash.: Northwest Association of Schools and Colleges, 1992.

Southern Association of Colleges and Schools (SACS), Commission on Colleges. *Criteria for Accreditation*. Atlanta, Ga.: Southern Association of Colleges and Schools, 1992.
Thompson, J. D. *Organizations in Action*. New York: McGraw-Hill, 1967.
Western Association of Schools and Colleges (WASC), Commission for Senior Colleges and Universities. *Handbook of Accreditation*. Oakland, Calif.: Western Association of Schools and Colleges, 1988.

SANDRA E. ELMAN is associate director of the Commission on Institutions of Higher Education, New England Association of Schools and Colleges.

Index

AAUP. *See* American Association of University Professors

Academic freedom: and AAUP 1915 declaration, 79–85; and AAUP 1940 statement, 83–85; and academic responsibility, 7–8; academics' indifference to, 2; and accreditation, 7, 89–99; and artistic expression, 5; and classroom, 12, 18; and collegial judgment, 2, 7; comprehensive, everyday view of, 1; and curriculum development, 12, 94, 97; departures from, 11–12; and "dirty little cases" (study), 59–73; and effective education, 11; elements of, 80; and extraprofessional matters, 77, 80–81; and faculty assessment, 12, 15–17; and faculty discourse, 5–6, 22; and federal policy, 2, 15; and First Amendment, 23, 24, 26, 28, 81, 84, 85; and fiscal constraint, 2–3, 12–13, 18; and governance, 5–6, 59–73, 97–99; justification for, 79–80; limits on, 96; and professional ethics/behavior, 7, 12, 22, 27; public benefit of, 82; and research, 4–5, 33–43; and sexual harassment, 21–30; of speech, 7, 22, 28, 55, 77–86; and speech codes, 12, 13–15; and student-teacher relationship, 93; and subject matter/ideology, 3; and teaching, 11–18; and tenure, 8, 86; and truth, 55; types of, 12; and unprofessional behavior, 8, 30

"Academic Freedom and Artistic Expression," 49, 50, 51, 57

"Academic Freedom and Sexual Harassment," 29

Academic freedom cases. *See* "Dirty little cases"

Academic governance. *See* Governance

Accreditation: and academic freedom, 7, 89–99; and assessment movement, 17; and curriculum development, 94; debate about role of, 89; democratic nature of, 97; and diversity, 89–90, 94; goal of, 95; and institutional mission, 91; and physical resources, 98–99; and planning/evaluation, 97; regional, 91, 97–98; standards, 91–93, 97; and student competencies, 95–96; and student outcomes assessment, 90, 94–96

Alvernia College, 66–67

American Association of Higher Education, 16

American Association of University Professors (AAUP), 50–51, 59, 61, 63–70, 73, 80, 82–83

American Medical Association, 33, 34

Andersen, K. E., 18

Angelo, T., 16

"Arbitration in Cases of Dismissal," 27

Artistic expression: challenges to, 45; controversial, 46, 49; cultural/political significance of, 56; and federal funding, 48–49; feminists complaints about, 53; and hecklers, 50; Illinois Community College (case example), 51; and institutional disclaimers, 52; and institutional mission, 50; and institutional neutrality, 49–50, 52; legal limitations on, 52; legislation restricting, 47; and low art, 53; Northwestern University (case example), 54; and obscenity, 47–48; performative dimension of, 47; and place of display, 51; political significance of, 55–56; and pornography, 56; power of, 55; protests about, 46; regulation of, 51, 57; and regulatory balance, 52–55, 57; San Francisco State University (case example), 46; and scholarly publication, 56–57; and sexual harassment, 46; and teachers, 45, 56–57; University of Michigan Law School (case example), 53; Vanderbilt University (case example), 46; Wolf Trap statement on, 50–52

Arts: and academic freedom, 55–57; and censorship, 47, 50; federal funding of, 48–49; and Republican administrations, 48; role of, in higher education, 57

Assessment: and academic freedom, 15; and accreditation, 17; American Association of Higher Education conference on, 16–17; and course evaluations, 15–16; and educational effectiveness, 15; and eductional objectives, 96; and external agencies, 96; faculty, 12; goal

Assessment (*continued*)
  of, 95; government involvement in, 15; and innovation, 95; legal implications of, 15; movement, 16; process of, 95; and resources, 17; skepticism about, 95; student outcomes, 90, 94–96
Association of Women in Mathematics, 24
Ayoub v. *Texas A & M University*, 78

Ballard v. *Blount*, 78
Benjamin, E., 4, 15
Bergmann, B. R., 18
Bishop v. *Arnov et al.*, 26
Board of Regents v. *Roth*, 79
Bostick, A., 46
Brewster, K., Jr., 1
Byrne, P., 80

Caplow, T., 72
Carnegie Commission on Higher Education, 62
Censorship: in arts, 47–52; and federal funding, 48–49; and obscenity, 47–48; and religious beliefs, 48, 49; and scholarly research, 57
Cigarette advertising, and academic freedom (case study), 33–40
City University of New York (CUNY), 61
Civil Rights Act of 1964 (Title VII), 22
Claflin College, 78, 83
Clark, B. R., 71
Classroom: academic freedom in, 18, 93; atmosphere in, 24, 29; controls in, 12
Coleman, J. C., 14
College of Osteopathic Medicine and Surgery, 78
Committee A on Academic Freedom and Tenure, American Association of University Professors, 55, 63, 64, 65, 66, 67, 68, 69
Conflict: and professionalization theory, 72; and restructuring, 68
"Conflict About Art, A," 46
Connick v. *Myers*, 85
Curriculum: development by faculty, 94, 98; review of, 97–98

"Dirty little cases": Alvernia College (case example), 66–67; characteristics/context of, 61–63; and elite vs. non-elite schools, 69, 71–72; and factionalization, 61, 72; factors leading to, 73; and faculty autonomy/self-governance, 60, 72; and faculty subordination, 60, 69–70; Hillsdale College (case example), 66; Illinois College of Optometry (case example), 64–65; Laredo Community College (case example), 63–64; and locally oriented schools, 69; main points concerning, 60–61; and paternalistic administration, 69–70; and power imbalance, 60–61, 71–72; and professionalization theory, 59–60, 71–72; Talladega College (case example), 65; and tenure, 63, 73; and two- and four-year schools, 69, 72; University of Northern Colorado (case example), 67–69
Diversity, intrainstitutional, 89–90, 94
Dorsett v. *Board of Trustees*, 78, 79, 85
Douglas, J. M., 70

Elman, S. E., 91
Elmira Collge, 78, 83
Emory University, 13, 15
Ethics: and course presentation, 12; and faculty behavior, 22; professional, of faculty, 7, 12, 22, 25; and prohibitions on speech, 26; of students, 22
Etzioni, A., 60, 71

Faculty: and academic values, 40; African-American, 65; art, 45, 50, 56–57; assessment of, 15–17; autonomy of, 60; collective action by, 60–61, 70–72; control of policies, 18; and course evaluation, 15–16; and curriculum development, 94, 98; dating of students by, 23; and "dirty little cases" (study), 59–73; disciplining, 21, 27; discourse of, 5–6, 22; and educational policy, 78, 83–86; ethics of, 7, 12, 22, 25; extramural speech of, 80–81; factionalization of, 61, 72; as gods, 22–23; and governance, 5–6, 59–73, 82–83; intramural speech of, 77–86; and leaders, 40; legal action by, 70–71; and mission, 7; multidimensional role of, 93; nonprofessional vs. professional speech of, 81–82; peer review of, 82; personal comments by, 23–24; personal views of, 26; and physical resources planning, 98–99; planning role of, 98; and power imbalances, 60–61, 71–72; and process theory, 60, 71–72; and program review, 97–98; relationship with students, 93;

research of, 4–5, 33–40; responsibilities of, 7, 21, 29–30; and restructuring, 68–69; role of, 82–84; and scholarly goals, 18; sexual harassment by, 22–23; subordination of, 60, 69–70; and trait theory, 60, 71; unprofessional behavior of, 8, 30
Feminists: and nude in art, 53; and pornography, 28
Finken, M., 3, 81
First Amendment, 23, 24, 26, 28, 30, 46, 55, 81, 84, 85
Fitzgerald, L. F., 13
"Formal Procedures for Handling Complaints of Discriminatory Harassment," 15
"Freedom and Tenure in the Academy," 3
Friedson, E., 60

Gouldner, A. W., 66
Governance: and academic freedom, 5–6, 59–73, 97–99; and collective action, 70–72; defined, 59; and "dirty little cases" (study), 59–73; faculty participation in, 5–6, 59–73, 82–83; and intramural speech, 82; and power bases, 72; and professionalization theory, 59–60, 71–72; and restructuring, 69
Greenwood, E., 60
Gross, B. R., 14

Halfond, J. A., 18
Harassment: and academic discourse, 22; faculty responsibilities regarding, 21, 29–30; and hostile classroom atmosphere, 22, 24, 29; and reasonable student/faculty member standard, 21–22, 25–26; and speech codes, 13–14, 21; student-to-student, 22; targeted vs. untargeted, 29; workplace, 22. *See also* Sexual harassment
Higher education: artist's role in, 48; arts in, 57; assessment of, 15; diversity in, 89–90; effectiveness of, 11, 15; external intrusion into, 18; and faculty assessment, 15–17; and faculty control of goals/policies, 18; institutional mission of, 50, 91; movements constraining, 12–13; physical resource planning in, 98–99; planning in, 98–99; restructuring of, 68; and scholarly goals, 18; and speech codes, 13–15
Hillsdale College, 66

Hogan, R., 17
Honan, W. H., 14

Idoux v. *Lamar University System,* 79
Illinois College of Optometry, 64–65
Illinois Community College, 51
Instruction. *See* Teaching
Intramural speech: and AAUP 1915 declaration, 79–85; and AAUP 1940 statement, 83–85; and academic freedom, 79–82, 84, 86; and academic standards, 78–79; and administrative issues, 79; and budgetary issues, 79; disputes involving, 77–79; and educational policy issues, 78, 83–86; and extramural speech, 81; and governance, 82; policy and legal doctrine on, 84–85; specific issues on, 77–78; Supreme Court rulings on, 84–85

Jacobs, L. A., 14
Jeffries v. *Harleston,* 78, 85
Jencks, C., 72
Johnson v. *Lincoln University,* 79, 85

Kent, P. A., 39
Kerr, C., 72
Keyishian v. *Board of Regents,* 85
Kurtz v. *Vickrey,* 78, 79

Landrum v. *Eastern Kentucky University,* 78, 85
Laredo Community College, 63–64
Larson, M. S., 60
Leachman v. *Rector & Visitors,* 79
Lees College, 78
Leonard, R., 13
Levin, G., 35
Longanecker, D. A., 15

McDonald, M. P., 17
McGee, R. J., 72
Mathematics, and sexual harassment, 24–25
Medical College of Georgia (MCG), 34–40
Metzger, W. P., 60
Middle States Association of Colleges and Schools (MSACS), 91, 92, 93
Minnesota State Board for Community Colleges v. *Knight,* 78, 84
Mission: and artistic expression, 50; faculty role in, 7; institutional, and accreditation, 91, 96

Moore, W. E., 60
Mount Ida College, 78, 83

Naramanchi v. *Board of Trustees,* 78
National Center for Education Statistics, 70
National Endowment for the Arts, 48, 49
National Endowment for the Humanities, 48
National Labor Relations Board v. *Yeshiva University,* 67, 83
New England Association of Schools and Colleges (NEASC), 91, 92, 94, 96, 97, 98, 99
Newsletter of the Association for Women in Mathematics, 24
"1940 Statement of Principles on Academic Freedom and Tenure," 5, 7, 21, 56, 83
North Central Association of Colleges and Schools (NCACS), 91
North Greenville College, 78, 79, 82
Northwest Association of Schools and Colleges (NASC), 91, 92
Northwestern University, 53, 54

Obscenity, in arts, 48
"On the Relationship of Faculty Governance to Academic Freedom," 6, 85
O'Neill, R. M., 47
Onondaga Community College, 78, 79
Or, B. G., 70

Pairowski v. *Illinois Community College,* 51
Parsons, C., 46
Perry v. *Sindermann,* 78
Phelan, P., 48
Philander Smith College, 79
Poch, R. K., 52
Political correctness, 15
Power: faculty-administration, imbalances, 60–61, 71–72; and governance, 72; and process theory, 72; and sexual harassment, 21, 24, 29–30
Professionalization theory: and elite vs. non-elite schools, 71–72; and intra-institutional conflict, 72; and power imbalances, 71–72; process school of, 60, 71–72; schools of, 59; trait school of, 60, 71; and unionization, 72
Professors. *See* Faculty

R.J. Reynolds Tobacco Company, 33–40
Rabban, D. M., 80, 85
"Recommended Institutional Regulations on Academic Freedom and Tenure," 8, 30
Regents of University of Michigan v. *Ewing,* 84, 85
Reisman, D., 72
Research: controversial, 5; freedom of faculty, 4–5; tobacco advertising, and academic freedom (case study), 33–40
Retrenchment/restructuring, and governance, 68–69
Rorty, A. O., 81

Salemi, J. S., 15
"San Francisco State Destroys Malcolm X Mural After Furor," 46
San Francisco State University, 46
Searle, J. R., 81
Sexual harassment: and academic detachment, 25; academic freedom without, 29–30; and artistic expression, 46; and Civil Rights Act of 1964, 22; and course content, 27; and dating of students by faculty, 23; and disciplinary measures, 27; and explicit comments, 24; by faculty, 22–23; forms of, 24; and gays/lesbians, 23; and general comments, 24; in mathematics, 24–25; parameters of, 23–26; and personal comments, 23–24; and personal opinion, 26; and power, 21, 24, 29–30; and relevant course material, 27; as sexual discrimination, 22, 23; and Title VII, 22; and workplace context, 22
Shils, E., 2, 6, 55
Silva, E. T., 72
Slaughter, S., 61, 68, 69, 72
Smith, M.L.A., 63
Southern Association of Colleges and Schools (SACS), 91, 92
Speech: and academic discourse, 5–6, 22; and academic freedom, 7, 22; extramural, 81; and First Amendment, 23, 24, 26, 28, 81, 84, 85; intramural, 77–86; political, 55; professional vs. nonprofessional, 81–82. *See also* Intramural speech; Speech codes
Speech codes: absurd basis of, 13; and academic freedom, 12, 13–15; and con-

troversial topics, 15; disruptiveness of, 14; genesis of, 13; and harassment, 13–14; and political correctness, 15; and sexual harassment, 29
"Statement of the Association's Council," 21
"Statement on Government of Colleges and Universities," 6, 82–83
"Statement on Professional Ethics," 6, 21
Stern, C. S., 48
Student learning outcomes assessment, 90, 94–96
Students: abuse of, 21; competencies of, 95–96; faculty challenging of, 26; faculty dating of, 23; freedom of, 4; teacher relationship with, 93
"Symposium on Academic Freedom," 3

Talladega College, 65, 78, 79, 83–84
Teachers. *See* Faculty
Teaching: and academic freedom, 11–13; and ancillary instruction, 12–13; aspects of, 12–13; and basis of understanding, 12–13; constraints on, 12–13; and course content, 12–13; and personal opinion, 26
Tenure: and academic freedom, 8, 86; and "dirty little cases," 63, 73; disputes involving, 78
Thernstrom, S., 14
Thoades, G., 70
Thompson, J. D., 97
Tobacco companies, and medical research (case study), 34–40
Tobin, R. W., 15

Unionization/collective action: faculty, 60–61, 63, 71–72; and power imbalances, 60–61, 71–72; professionalization theory and, 72
University of Michigan Law School, 53
University of Northern Colorado, 67–69

Van Alstyne, W., 80, 85
Vanderbilt University, 46

Warren, D. L., 15
Wesley College, 78, 79, 82
Western Association of Schools and Colleges (WASC), 91, 92
"Who Controls the Researcher's Files?" 35–36
Wirsig, M. E., 17
Wolf Trap Conference of American Association of University Professors, 50–52

Ordering Information

NEW DIRECTIONS FOR HIGHER EDUCATION is a series of paperback books that provides timely information and authoritative advice about major issues and administrative problems confronting every institution. Books in the series are published quarterly in Spring, Summer, Fall, and Winter and are available for purchase by subscription and individually.

SUBSCRIPTIONS for 1994 cost $47.00 for individuals (a savings of 30 percent over single-copy prices) and $62.00 for institutions, agencies, and libraries. Please do not send institutional checks for personal subscriptions. Standing orders are accepted.

SINGLE COPIES cost $16.95 when payment accompanies order. (California, New Jersey, New York, and Washington, D.C., residents please include appropriate sales tax.) All orders will be charged shipping and handling.

DISCOUNTS FOR QUANTITY ORDERS are available. Please write to the address below for information.

ALL ORDERS must include either the name of an individual or an official purchase order number. Please submit your order as follows:
   Subscriptions: specify series and year subscription is to begin
   Single copies: include individual title code (such as HE82)

MAIL ALL ORDERS TO:
   Jossey-Bass Publishers
   350 Sansome Street
   San Francisco, California 94104-1342

FOR SUBSCRIPTION SALES OUTSIDE OF THE UNITED STATES, contact any international subscription agency or Jossey-Bass directly.

OTHER TITLES AVAILABLE IN THE
NEW DIRECTIONS FOR HIGHER EDUCATION SERIES
Martin Kramer, Editor-in-Chief

HE87 Developing Administrative Excellence: Creating a Culture of Leadership, *Sharon A. McDade, Phyllis H. Lewis*
HE86 Total Quality Management on Campus: Is It Worth Doing? *Daniel Seymour*
HE85 America's Investment in Liberal Education, *David H. Finifter, Arthur M. Hauptman*
HE84 Strengthening the College Major, *Carol Geary Schneider, William Scott Green*
HE83 Financial Management: Progress and Challenges, *William E. Vandament, Dennis P. Jones*
HE82 Important Lessons from Innovative Colleges and Universities, *V. Ray Cardozier*
HE81 Recognizing Faculty Work: Reward Systems for the Year 2000, *Robert M. Diamond, Bronwyn E. Adam*
HE80 Assessment and Curriculum Reform, *James L. Ratcliff*
HE79 Agendas for Church-Related Colleges and Universities, *David S. Guthrie, Richard L. Noftzger, Jr.*
HE78 Information Literacy: Developing Students as Independent Learners, *D. W. Farmer, Terrence F. Mech*
HE77 The Campus and Environmental Responsibility, *David J. Eagan, David W. Orr*
HE76 Administration as a Profession, *Jonathan D. Fife, Lester F. Goodchild*
HE75 Faculty in Governance: The Role of Senates and Joint Committees in Academic Decision Making, *Robert Birnbaum*
HE74 The Changing Dimensions of Student Aid, *Jamie P. Merisotis*
HE73 Using Consultants Successfully, *Jon F. Wergin*
HE72 Administrative Careers and the Marketplace, *Kathryn M. Moore, Susan B. Twombly*
HE71 Managing Change in Higher Education, *Douglas W. Steeples*
HE70 An Agenda for the New Decade, *Larry W. Jones, Franz A. Nowotny*
HE69 Financial Planning Under Economic Uncertainty, *Richard E. Anderson, Joel W. Meyerson*
HE67 Achieving Assessment Goals Using Evaluation Techniques, *Peter J. Gray*
HE64 Successful Strategic Planning: Case Studies, *Douglas W. Steeples*
HE62 Making Computers Work for Administrators, *Kenneth C. Green, Steven W. Gilbert*
HE61 Leaders on Leadership: The College Presidency, *James L. Fisher, Martha W. Tack*
HE60 Increasing Retention: Academic and Student Affairs Administrators in Partnership, *Martha McGinty Stodt, William M. Klepper*
HE59 Student Outcomes Assessment: What Institutions Stand to Gain, *Diane F. Halpern*
HE45 Women in Higher Education Administration, *Adrian Tinsley, Cynthia Secor, Sheila Kaplan*